ARTHA

GOLFO DE L'ARTHA

S. GEORGIO

BASILIO

S. NICOLO

CHRYSO

VATHI

BREVESSA

VONISA

TENPIO D'APOLLINE

SENO

AMBRACIO

S. MAVRE

LEVCADIA

St. Jeames

parke

Charinge

Tootehill streete

G

H

Scotland

N

D

White

E

Prevye sta

Sanctuary

A

Garden stayres

Oldpallace

The pallace

The Riuer

B

Kinges bridge

Iyll banke

The Q. slaugh ter howse
The myll

Old pallace bridge

Stanegate stayres

Lambet

ambeth stayres

Mapping Shakespeare's World

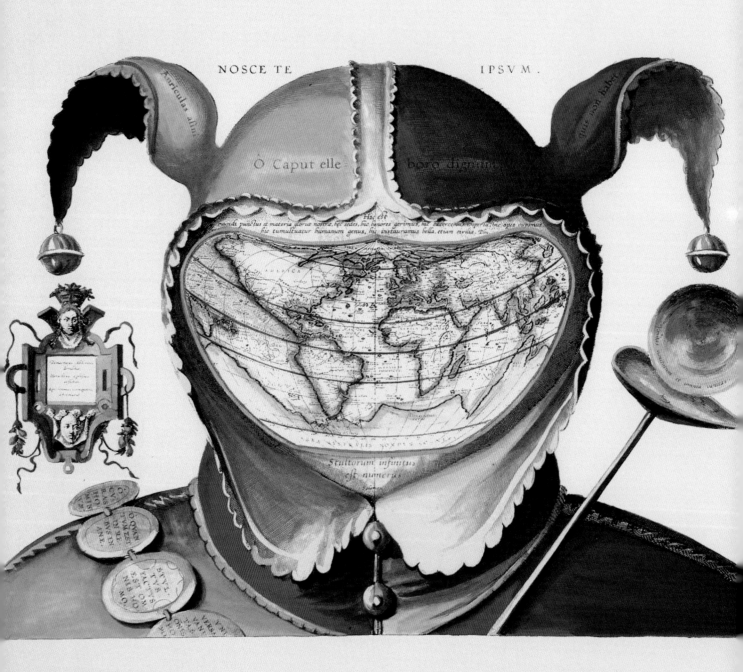

Mapping Shakespeare's World

PETER WHITFIELD

Bodleian Library
UNIVERSITY OF OXFORD

First published in 2015 by the Bodleian Library
Broad Street
Oxford OX1 3BG

www.bodleianshop.co.uk

ISBN 978 1 85124 257 3

Text © Peter Whitfield, 2015
Images, unless specified on page 192,
© Bodleian Library, University of Oxford, 2015

Cover design by Dot Little
Designed and typeset in 11½ on 16 Garamond
by illuminati, Grosmont
Printed and bound by Prosperous Printing Co. Ltd, China
on FSC® certified 128 gsm Neo Matt

British Library Catalogue in Publishing Data
A CIP record of this publication is available from the British Library

FRONTISPIECE *The Fool's Cap World*, anonymous, *c.* 1590; a well-known
and eloquent image of the world as a fool or a madman, a conception
which Shakespeare would echo, and which might be seen as a direct
inspiration for certain passages in *King Lear*.

ENDPAPERS Details from FIG. 23, the naval Battle of Preveza;
and FIG. 95, Norden's Map of Westminster of 1593.

Contents

POLY-OLBION

GREAT BRITAINE

By
Michaell Drayton
Esqr:

London printed for { M. Lownes. I. Browne. Engraue
I. Helme. I. Busbie. by W. Hole.

PRELIMINARY

Maps of man & the cosmos

'There is a world elsewhere'—*Coriolanus*[1]

THE WHOLE OF Shakespearean drama is in a sense encapsulated in that simple phrase, and it is a striking fact that Shakespeare never wrote a play that was explicitly set in the world in which he lived, Elizabethan London. All his plays are located in settings remote in space or time from the England which he and his audiences inhabited, faraway places where the imagination could be set free, where anything could happen. It has often been argued that no matter where the plays were set, Shakespeare was writing about his own culture and his own time, because his true theme was human life as he perceived it, and that the overt settings are superficial details that tell us nothing about what is happening in these dramas. In this view, whatever we are nominally looking at on stage – ancient Britain, Mediterranean islands, medieval France, imperial Rome, Renaissance Italy – the real setting is simply Elizabethan London, the same everyday world that the audience meets outside the doors of the theatre. I disagree with this approach, because it implies that the plays' settings are, in the last resort, meaningless fictions, that any location is as good as another, and I cannot believe that this is a rational position.

All places exist in the imagination as much as in reality, perhaps even more in the imagination than in reality. We all share the images of a thousand places which we have never seen – of Venice or New York, the walls of Troy or the Parthenon, the deserts of Arabia or the paradise islands of the Pacific. These images are not merely pictures of what a place looks like, but a sense

1 *Poly-Olbion*, 1612: the title page to Drayton's epic description of England and Wales. The image shows Britannia robed in a map, surrounded by the wealth of land and sea, and the armed figures who guard it.

of its inner character, its people and its atmosphere. And even when we have been to Venice, lured there by the legend of its unique beauty, and have been appalled by the tourist crowds and pronounced the place irretrievably spoiled, still the Canaletto image of a graceful but slightly decadent city remains intact in our dream-memory, insulated from reality. Therefore when the action of a play opens in Venice or Rome, Sicily or Denmark, in an ancient pagan land or in the England of a hundred years ago, we already have some feelings, some expectations, imagined possibilities and limitations, about what we are about to see. I don't think there is any doubt that Shakespeare also had such feelings. He lived within a mature literary and intellectual tradition, which included a strong awareness of geography and history; why should we imagine him to be cut off from a sense of place, time and setting?

The setting is surely one element, and an important one, in the imaginative genesis of a literary work. 'I have read everything', the ebullient young Coleridge said once; and perhaps he had, but he had not been everywhere, and a vast amount of what he had read ended up in poems like 'Kubla Khan' and *The Rime of the Ancient Mariner*, which take us to the remotest regions of the world. In *The Road to Xanadu*, the American scholar John Livingston Lowes wrote an intricate and convincing study of the way that Coleridge's reading entered his poems, and the road of Lowes's research led him 'through half the lands and all the seven seas of the globe'.[2] Lowes's considered conclusion was that 'the imagination works its wonders through the exercise, in the main, of normal and intelligible powers', and that principle applies to all writers. The imagination is a transforming power, but clearly there must be something for it to transform. Shakespeare, as far as we know, hadn't been everywhere either; in fact he may not have been anywhere at all outside southern England. But he too had 'read everything', or at least everything he needed to give him the framework to say what he had to say, including within that framework a basis for the locations.

Consider these lines from *Much Ado About Nothing*: Benedick, wishing to escape the presence of Beatrice, does not say to Don Pedro 'Can I go away for a while?' He says:

Will your grace command me any service to the world's end? I will
go on the slightest errand now to the Antipodes that you can devise
to send me on; I will fetch you a toothpicker now from the furthest

2 London from the Sheldon Tapestry map of Oxfordshire. A vivid testimony to a new English interest in maps, these astonishing tapestries were woven around 1590, possibly in Warwickshire.

FINCHLEY
HORNSEY
HIGAT
HAMPSTED
NEWINGTON
ISLINGTON
HAKENEY
PADDINGTON
S·GILES
ACTON
KENGINGTON
LONDON
HAMERSMITH
LAMBETH
CHELSY
SOUTHWAR
CHISWICKE
FVLHAM
NEWI

inch of Asia; bring you the length of Prester John's foot; fetch you
a hair off the great Cham's beard; do you any embassage to the
Pigmies, rather than hold three words conference with this harpy.[3]

This is the clearest possible proof of Shakespeare's knowledge of the
literature of medieval and Renaissance geography, from Marco Polo to
Hakluyt, and here that knowledge is turned vividly into a comic conceit.

A second example: the death of the Duke of Norfolk in *Richard II* is
reported in these terms:

> Many a time hath banish'd Norfolk fought
> For Jesu Christ in glorious Christian field,
> Streaming the ensign of the Christian cross
> Against black pagans, Turks and Saracens;
> And toil'd with works of war, retir'd himself
> To Italy; and there at Venice gave
> His body to that pleasant country's earth,
> And his pure soul unto his captain Christ,
> Under whose colours he had fought so long.[4]

In compressed form, these few lines convey the English image of the
crusades accepted in Shakespeare's day: the Christian knight battling
in the burning sun of Palestine – in this case to expiate some personal
guilt – then finally retiring to the beauty of Italy, which was also the
heartland of Christendom, to resign his life. Like Benedick's words, they
embody considerable geographical and historical feeling for events of which
Shakespeare himself had no direct knowledge. In other words, there is a
presumption that some thought and some feeling went into the locations
of Shakespeare's plays, that they were chosen to be at the very least fitting,
if not always deeply significant or symbolic in some way, and that part of
that choice was the perceived character of any given place.

This book sets out to survey the settings of the Shakespeare plays, to
ask how familiar they were, or what they might have meant to Shakespeare
himself and his contemporaries. It also maps Shakespeare's visual world
in a more general sense, looking at historical events, historical figures and
cultural stereotypes associated with those places. These are all things which
Shakespeare would undoubtedly have been aware of from his study of those

texts which inspired the plays, texts to which he returned again and again: Ovid, Plutarch, Boccaccio and Holinshed. Many of these places and events were also the subject of illustrations, and, for us today, these texts and their illustrations can play an important part in leading us into the settings in which the plays take place. It is true that many of the locations in Shakespeare's plays were given in his sources, and that he did not often change them. Some of these places – Rome or Venice for example – would have already possessed distinct identities. But most of them would not: what did Messina, Navarre, Elsinore or Verona mean to people in Elizabethan England? Not a great deal perhaps, except to the educated few, but in many such cases it would be Shakespeare's plays which gave these locations an identity, in the meta-life which the plays enjoyed over the centuries following their first performance.

The world of Shakespeare's plays has three great divisions, which are spatial, temporal and cultural. The first is the world of Greece and Rome, clearly an ancient world, but one which shades into Shakespeare's own time through the presence of the Mediterranean background. It is the Mediterranean which links *The Tempest*, *Othello* and *The Merchant of Venice* with *Pericles*, *The Comedy of Errors* and *Antony and Cleopatra*. The second division is the world of Renaissance Europe, the cities and the courts, scattered from Sicily to Denmark, where many of the great comedies and two of the tragedies are set. Then thirdly there is Britain, ancient and medieval, legendary and historical. These were all 'worlds elsewhere', displayed by Shakespeare to his London theatre audiences, used by him to explore human psychology, and to show the transformations wrought by passion, by comedy and by suffering. We must conclude that Shakespeare felt he could not achieve this through dramas located in the everyday world of his own era. Instead he gives us a series of worlds, linked only by the fact of being essentially European, into which Asia, Africa and the Americas send only a few faint echoes. This book will move geographically across these regions, from the Eastern Mediterranean to Western and Northern Europe, and from the ancient world to sixteenth-century England. It will also move through successive geographical categories, focusing at various times on ideas of the cosmos, of the whole world, of Europe, of Britain, and of London.

The idea of mapping Shakespeare's world is particularly apposite, since the Tudor age witnessed a heightened awareness in England of maps as significant

DIEV ET MON DROIT

GRONLAN

TROPICVS

THE SOUTH

TROPICVS

SEA

VIRGINIA

BRASILIA

PERV

GVIANA

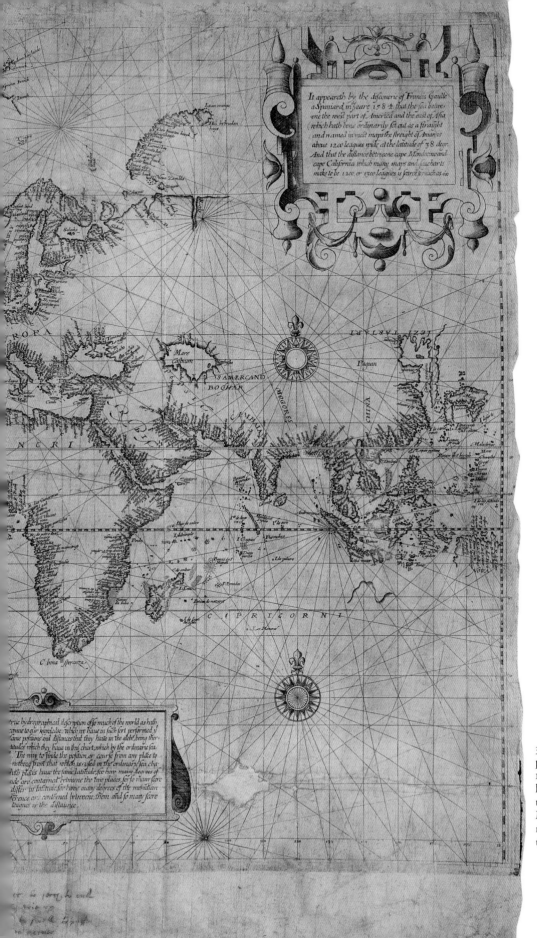

3 World Map by Edward Wright, published in Hakluyt's *Voyages* in 1600. The maze of navigational lines are believed to have inspired the lines in *Twelfth Night* where Malvolio's face is likened to 'the new map with the augmentation of the Indies'.

intellectual and political documents. By the early 1500s, Italy and Germany had developed sophisticated traditions of mapping cities and regions, charting the seas and coasts, and publishing collections of maps, known as atlases, while no such activity had even begun in Britain. A hundred years later, however, the situation was very different, with home-produced and imported maps now familiar and valued tools in the hands of the traveller, the statesman, the soldier and the scholar. The map was an interpretation of the world, an ordering of space, which conferred power on those who possessed it. It was also an object of delight to the eye, as were topographical views of cities – London, Paris, Venice, Rome – where one seemed to hover over the city with the all-seeing gaze of a god. In public consciousness, the Tudor revolution in cartography probably reached its culmination in the county maps of Christopher Saxton, first published in 1579, which made England overnight into the best-mapped nation in Europe, and which gave Englishmen a distinct new image of their land, superbly detailed and artistically inspiring.

That Shakespeare was fully aware of this cartographic revolution appears from a number references in the plays to travel and exploration. More specifically, there are two occasions on which Shakespeare introduces a map into his dramas. In part one of *Henry IV*, the rebel earls who are planning to topple the new king produce a map of England and confidently set about dividing the country between them. One of them, Hotspur, thinks his territory is too small, and proposes to use gunpowder to blast the River Trent into a new course, in order to enlarge his share. Some years later when he came to write *King Lear*, Shakespeare again calls for a map on stage, to be used by the ageing king when he divides his kingdom among his three daughters. It is a fair guess that Shakespeare imitated this idea from Marlowe's *Tamburlaine*, where the dying warrior had also called for a map, which must have shown most of the known world, in order to trace the scenes of his former triumphs in Asia and Africa, but also to lament over the other regions of the earth with the words 'And shall I die, and this unconquered?'[5] The only place where Shakespeare seems to mention a specific contemporary map comes in *Twelfth Night*, where Malvolio's smiling face is likened to a world map criss-crossed with compass lines; in 1599 just such a map, drawn by Edward Wright, had been published with Hakluyt's *Voyages*, and scholars have conjectured that the dramatist had this very map in mind. In *The Comedy of Errors*, no map is produced on stage, but Dromio of Syracuse compares Nell, the fat kitchen maid, to a globe of the world, and develops an extended metaphor of her body as a map. These examples show that Shakespeare had recognized that maps could be a source of novel and arresting imagery.

But geography in the familiar sense was only one aspect of maps, for there were also other kinds of maps which located mankind within the universal realm, and claimed to codify the invisible links between mankind and nature. In the later seventeenth century, in the age of the new science, these maps would become swiftly extinct, but in their various forms they had already left a large imprint on Shakespeare's works. Scholars have often pointed out how difficult it is to pinpoint Shakespeare's intellectual beliefs about subjects such as religion, science and philosophy. For example, the dramatist lived and wrote in the aftermath of one of the greatest intellectual revolutions in history – the Copernican Revolution, which argued that the Earth was not the centre of the cosmos, but a planet orbiting the sun. This overturned long centuries of belief in the Ptolemaic system, in which the planets and all the stars revolved around the Earth in a finite mechanism under the control of God. This was the belief underwritten by the Roman Catholic Church and given classic expression in Dante's *The Divine Comedy*. The new system proposed by Copernicus was long in winning acceptance, and Donne responded to the uncertainty it created with the words 'And new philosophy calls all in doubt'.[6] In Shakespeare we find no direct reference to theories of the heavens, but perhaps this should not surprise us so very much. In our own time, if we think of Edwin Hubble's work leading to the discovery of the expanding universe in the early 1930s, how much impact did that have on the theatre of the interwar years, or indeed of any period afterwards? Even Marlowe, a more overtly intellectual writer who delighted in showing off his learning, gives a clear account of the older Ptolemaic system in *Doctor Faustus*, but not of the new one. Here Faustus, with diabolic aid, is conveyed through the heavens 'to find the secrets of astronomy', travelling through the celestial spheres as Dante had done, although Faustus's journey certainly does not end in a beatific vision. A general understanding of the Copernican Revolution had to wait, and it emerged slowly over a period of more than a century.

4 (*overleaf*) Asia from the Desceliers' world map of 1550. With its vivid images of warlike kings and wild beasts, this map evokes perfectly the savage heart of Asia from which Marlowe's Tamburlaine erupted to conquer half the world.

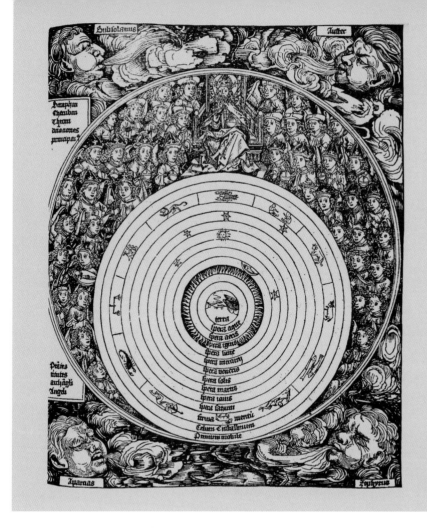

5 The Ptolemaic Universe, depicted in the *Nürnberg Chronicle*, 1493. The cosmos is divided into concentric spheres centred on the Earth, and the whole structure is turned by God and his angels; this is the system clearly described in Marlowe's *Doctor Faustus*.

Nevertheless this problem of the structure and nature of the cosmos is the scientific and philosophical question underlying all others; the map of the heavens is the primary map that has to be drawn in order to locate mankind in time and space. In a less scientific sense than in Marlowe, the heavens are present in many memorable passages in Shakespeare, used as symbols of universal order and disorder, and he represents the ancient, traditional belief that there is a fundamental link between the cosmos and mankind, that order or disorder in the first will produce order or disorder in the second. The clearest expression of this belief is found in *Troilus and Cressida*, in Ulysses' great speech on the hierarchy of nature, from the heavens down to the social life of men, a speech which strongly suggests that Shakespeare fully accepted the idea of a link between the universe and humanity, between the macrocosm and the microcosm. In *The Merchant of Venice*, Lorenzo voices a poetic account of the doctrine of the music of the spheres, music which mankind, locked in the imperfections of the flesh, cannot hear. Lear's great opening speech in the storm scene, 'Blow, winds, and crack your cheeks!',[7] is carefully structured to list uproar in the four classical elements in turn – air, water, fire and earth – with the clear message that this violence is linked to the chaos in Lear's mind.

These are all clues to Shakespeare's conception of nature and man's organic place within it. But in fact the most familiar expression of that relationship is to be found in the doctrines of astrology, which formed the most fully articulated scientific system of the Middle Ages and the Renaissance. Astrology provided a series of maps of the relationships between heavenly and earthly things, maps which served to locate man

6 The Astrological Universe, a counterpart to the Ptolemaic, showing the houses, the zodiac signs and the planets, ruled by God and pouring their invisible influences down upon the Earth. Illustration by Holbein from an astrological treatise by Leonhard Reynmann, 1515.

within the universe just as the Ptolemaic diagram of the cosmos had done. The central idea was that the celestial bodies – sun, moon, planets and zodiac constellations – radiated influences which shaped human character and earthly events, and this was elaborated into a complex system in which the positions of those bodies were carefully charted in order to interpret those influences. Astrology originated in the pagan era, but it made the transition into the Christian world through the belief that God was the ultimate power behind the celestial influences, that in effect he used the stars and planets as intermediaries in his rule over the universe.

The most familiar effects of those influences were physical: medieval and Renaissance medicine was unthinkable without astrology, and charts of the human body were drawn to show which parts were under the influence of which stars and planets. Shakespeare knew these diagrams (which were termed 'Zodiac Men'), and refers to them in *Twelfth Night*, although both Sir Andrew and Sir Toby get their details mixed up. Whether Shakespeare himself believed the astrological lore has been much discussed. He refers to it many times, usually with the implication that it is true, although this may of course be merely poetic rhetoric; but he puts the case against astrology most forcibly in Edmund's speech in *King Lear*[8] damning it all as a pure delusion.

Astrology was a special case of the doctrine of 'correspondences', the theory that all the divisions of the natural of world are linked to each other in their inner natures. Through the four elements, animals, plants, minerals, stars and planets may all interact with mankind in his spiritual and physical life. This doctrine was also the foundation for the art of magic, which claimed the power to manipulate these correspondences and to release their hidden powers, or even the personal spirits latent within them. Sixteenth-century scholars of the occult, such as Cornelius Agrippa and Tommaso Campanella, attempted to codify procedures and ceremonies which could compel natural substances to yield up their powers or spirits to do their bidding. The conjuring scene in part II of *Henry VI* shows the ceremony of raising a demon through the use of magic words and substances in order to extract a political prophecy from him. Marlowe portrayed such a magician in Faustus, and Shakespeare did the same in Prospero, but they are very different characters. Marlowe follows the late medieval morality tradition in showing Faustus as having gained his powers,

Fingitur Actæon noua fumere cornua cerui,
Dum videt & comites, & fine vefte Deam.

Scilicet ingenio confuefcunt effe feroci,
Quos nimium fyluæ, prædaq, capta iuuant.

Hie wirt gemeldt wie Diana
Macht zu eim Hirsch Acteona/

Welche mit Jagwerck vil gehn vmb/
Die werden gmeinglich wild vnd thumb.

Actæon

which were plainly evil, through a pact with the devil. Prospero's magic, however, consists in his power over nature and its personified spirits, which he has learned to control through a legitimate science, which was nonetheless real for being an occult science. Prospero's books, so feared by Caliban, would have included works by scholars like Agrippa, who systematized the ceremonies and magic formulae which released these powers. The final desperate words of Faustus before he is dragged down to hell, 'I'll burn my books', are surely echoed by the more humane Prospero when he promises of his own free will, 'I'll drown my book.'[9]

In Shakespeare's world, the invisible was at least as potent as the visible, and cosmology, astrology and magic had developed their maps and diagrams to interpret mankind's relationship to nature and the cosmos. Shakespeare was evidently aware of these traditions, which inhabit a borderland between science and a kind of pagan pantheism. Ovid's *Metamorphoses*, one of Shakespeare's favourite books, seems to spring from a similar cult of transformation, of man mingling his spirit and his flesh with the forms of nature, in this case through the will of the gods. To Renaissance writers and thinkers, the universe was not infinite, it was not empty and it was not impersonal or intrinsically hostile; instead it was hierarchical and purposeful, its parts interconnected in a way that might be thought of as forming a living whole.

7 Diana and Actaeon, from a German edition of Ovid's *Metamorphoses* published in 1569. The familiar image of Actaeon with a stag's head is almost certainly a source for Bottom's ass's head.

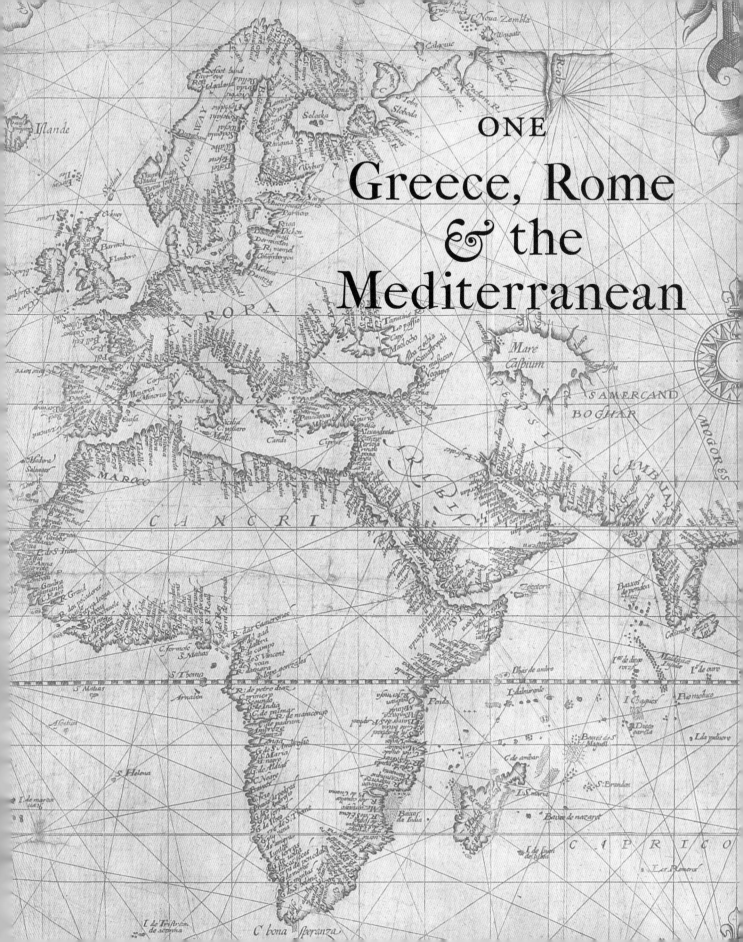

ONE

Greece, Rome & the Mediterranean

ETTOR

The Greek plays

THE PLAY REMOTEST in time and place from Shakespeare's England is *Troilus and Cressida*, the bleak, cynical story of love and betrayal that is set during the siege of Troy; that is, geographically in western Turkey, and conventionally regarded as taking place around 1000 BCE. Throughout the classical, medieval and Renaissance world, the story of the Trojan War had a unique status. It was seen as standing at the very beginning of secular history; it inaugurated the classical Greek era, and, through the figure of Aeneas, was the event from which the entire sweep of Roman history would flow; the account of it written by Homer stood at the beginning of European literature; the protagonists in that war were the greatest heroes of the Greek world, who contended not merely with each other, but with the gods; all the greatest and basest of human qualities – love, guilt, heroism, devotion, betrayal, revenge, cunning, fury, violence, honour, magnanimity – were displayed in it; the downfall of a great city and its civilization, brought about by guilty passion, bravery and pride combined, gave its story the archetypal resonance of a great tragedy; the Trojans who survived the destruction became the heroes of further legends concerning the founding of Rome, of Britain and of France. For two thousand years before Shakespeare lived, Troy had thus remained a major focus of narrative and visual art.

There was of course no precise knowledge of what Troy looked like, and no maps of it, but it is worth reminding ourselves that the site was not an abandoned ruin during those long centuries. Greek settlers began

8 Hector arming before going out to do battle with Achilles; drawing by Baldini, *c.*1470.

to occupy the site around 700 BCE, and a new city, now named Ilion, survived until the fourth century CE. The surrounding region of the Troas was ruled successively by the Persians, Alexander the Great, the Seleucid dynasty, the kingdom of Pergamum, and the Romans. In Roman times Ilion was extensively rebuilt, and was patronized as the supposed parent-city of Rome; it faded into obscurity only after the rise of Constantinople. This long post-Homeric history meant that there was continuous knowledge of the real, geographical Troy – it was never a lost or merely legendary city. When archaeologists of the nineteenth century took up the challenge of Troy, they knew exactly where to look – under the mound named by the Turks Hissarlik, and long known as the location of the Greek and Roman Ilion. There were other ancient stories about Troy not included in Homer, and these were taken up by writers of medieval romances, the key work being the French *Le Roman de Troie* by the twelfth-century author Benoît de Sainte-Maure. The love story of Troilus and Cressida was found here by Chaucer, and it was on Chaucer that Shakespeare chiefly drew for his narrative, and on another long poem, John Lydgate's *Troy Book*. Later,

9 *The Siege of Troy*, painting by Biagio di Antonio, *c*.1495. Troy was a favourite subject for medieval and Renaissance artists, and this elongated picture would have adorned the front of a *cassone*, the ornate wooden chests often presented as gifts.

a shortened version of Benoît's romance was translated into English and issued by Caxton in *c*.1474 as the first printed English book, *The Recuyell of the Histories of Troye.* Episodes from the Trojan War appeared in medieval art, illuminated manuscripts and tapestries. The besieged city, individual warriors in combat, and of course the Trojan horse, are all found, and these motifs were continued by Renaissance artists and book illustrators. It is entirely likely that Shakespeare had seen either the manuscripts, showing Troy as a towered and spired medieval city under siege, or pictures nearer to his own time, which conceived it in the Roman or contemporary Italian style. To an Elizabethan audience, Troy would have been a Graeco-Roman city in its appearance and its cultural identity.

Western Turkey and the seas of the Aegean and the Mediterranean, as far east as Cyprus and Syria, provide the background for two further plays set in an ancient world which is clearly Greek in character, but which is still more fabulous than Troy: *Pericles* and *The Comedy of Errors.* Both involve long and ill-fated sea voyages in the eastern Mediterranean, although in the case of *The Comedy of Errors* this has occurred offstage long before the

drama begins, and the play itself shows the ultimate consequences of that voyage – the comic resolution and reconciliation that follow years later. The action of *Pericles* also covers many years, but its scenes each take place before our eyes in real time, and this is, of all Shakespeare's plays, the richest in sea travel and its disasters, moving from coast to coast and involving danger, storm, shipwreck, separation, apparent death and resurrection, kidnapping and madness, before all is resolved. Antiochus, the evil king who initiates the action in *Pericles*, takes his name from a succession of Seleucid rulers of the third and second centuries BCE, whose territories included Syria and therefore Antioch. The background voyage in *The Comedy of Errors* was from Syracuse in Sicily to Ephesus, but the itinerary in *Pericles* is more complex, beginning on the coasts of Syria and taking in Antioch, Tyre and Tarsus, then moving further afield to Pentapolis and to the Aegean island of Mitylene, before ending too in Ephesus. Pentapolis

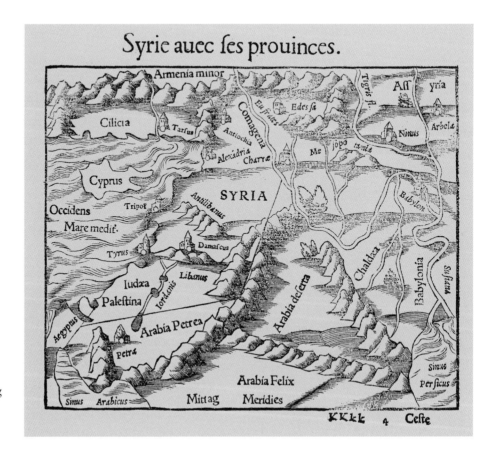

10 The coast of Syria, the setting of the first act of *Pericles*: Tyre, Antioch and Tarsus. From Münster's *Cosmographia*, 1552.

11 The island of Mytilene, site of the meeting of Pericles and Marina, mapped by Rosaccio in his *Viaggio da Venetia a Costantinopoli*, 1598.

was not a city but a region of north Africa, roughly corresponding to the Roman province of Cyrenaica; it included the five cities of Cyrene, Apollonia, Ptolemais, Berenice and Arsinoe. The others were well-known ports or cities which had survived from the ancient world, and were marked on all the Mediterranean sea charts of the sixteenth century, with the notable exception of Ephesus, long since ruined and abandoned. Since Ephesus is so important in both plays, it's worth asking what associations the city had. There would have been two significant ones, curiously contrasting.

First, it was associated with St Paul, and it played a major role in the historic progress of Christianity from Palestine to Rome. This explains why the city was always prominently marked on another kind of map which appeared in religious works and in atlases – the map of Paul's missionary journeys throughout the Mediterranean. The Christian community in Ephesus was one of the six young churches to receive lengthy epistles from St Paul, and it was one of the Asian churches addressed by St John in the Book of Revelation. St John's reputed tomb was in Ephesus, and in later traditions the Virgin Mary too lived and died there. Paul's epistle

Molem Asia immensam, faſtu ſpectanda ſuperbo   Sumptibus: inſano quæ vanus Eroſtratus aeſtu
Struxit, TEMPLA HECATES, regalibus vndiq̃ cincta   Incendit, ſtolidae venatus præmia famae.

12 The building of the Temple of Diana at Ephesus; print by Tempesta, 1608.

to the Ephesians is notable for its ethical teachings: Christian living in the relations between husbands and wives, parents and children, masters and servants, is the subject of religious reflection and exhortation. In the Roman play *Menaechmi* by Plautus, which was the literary model for *The Comedy of Errors*, the setting is given as the city of Epidamnus, and it must have been Shakespeare's own choice to change this to Ephesus. It seems possible that he did this in order to point up the connection between St Paul's morally edifying letter, and the manic twists and turns of human relationships portrayed in this riotous play. Ephesus was known as a centre of sorcery and the black arts, perhaps suggesting that the confusions of the play had some diabolic cause.

The other claim to fame that Ephesus possessed was something very different. What distinguished Ephesus from so many other ruined, abandoned classical cities was the memory of the great Temple of Diana, a truly colossal structure which was one of the seven wonders of the ancient world. Nominally the shrine of Diana or Artemis, here the goddess was realized in a bizarre, many-breasted form that had no connection with her familiar images, suggesting that the Ephesians had perpetuated the worship of some fertility goddess of the region, which had then become assimilated to the cult of Diana. The image of this strange, exotic Diana was familiar enough for Raphael to include it in his Vatican cycle of frescoes. The Ephesus temple measured some 50 by 150 metres, and the huge statue of the goddess was surrounded by a forest of more than 120 gigantic columns 20 metres in height. In 356 BCE, an earlier temple had been burned down by a madman, Herostratus, who reportedly sought worldwide fame by destroying that which was most famous throughout the world. The fire occurred on the very night that Alexander the Great was born. The temple was rebuilt with equal magnificence, and accounts of it are to be found in the works of many classical writers. In *Pericles* this is the temple to which Thaisa dedicates herself for many years after her rescue from the sea, and the place where she is reunited with Pericles and their daughter Marina.

Pericles belongs to the group of the four late romances, which centre on themes of destruction, loss, pain and separation, followed at last by reconciliation; they are dramas of death and rebirth, literal or metaphorical. All these plays can be seen as presenting a religious message, but their language is not Christian; it is pagan, with strong suggestions of magic and ceremonial healing – the sage who revives Thaisa is symbolically named Cerimon. For this purpose, what setting could be more appropriate than the greatest temple of the pagan goddess of the moon or of fertility? Pictures of Ephesus were familiar in the sixteenth and seventeenth centuries as one of the world's seven wonders, and Shakespeare could rely on something at least of the fame of the place resonating with his audience. That the same exotic, far-distant city should be used by Shakespeare for such different purposes in two very different plays, *The Comedy of Errors* being one of his very earliest and *Pericles* one of the latest, is both enigmatic and arresting. For one thing it refocuses our attention on *The Comedy of Errors*, which

13 Images of the very distinctive Ephesian Diana have been found in many parts of the Graeco-Roman world, this one in Rome; from de Bry's *Topographia Urbis Romae*, 1681.

ASSIA

14 Sea chart of the eastern Mediterranean drawn in Venice by Bartolomeo Olives, 1559. These charts were dense with place names on the coasts; the interiors were richly decorated with portraits of monarchs and vignettes of great cities like Venice and Cairo. Portolan charts were designed to be used at sea from any angle; the bottom of the page here is East.

15 Sea chart of the western
Mediterranean by Bartolomeo
Olives, Venice, 1559. Portolan
charts were designed to be
used at sea from any angle;
the bottom of the page here is
North.

AFRICA

EVROPA

Rey de Tunis

Rey de Feç

Rey de Tremiçen

Prinçipe de Spanya

Rey de Françia

Bartolomeo oliues mallorquina me fecit in veneçia a di 17 de junyo Año 1559

16 Map of St Paul's journey through the Mediterranean in Coverdale's New Testament of 1549, reaching from Syracuse to Ephesus, as in *The Comedy of Errors*.

turns out on reflection also to be a story of separation, rediscovery and healing, in which Emilia's reappearance anticipates that of Thaisa. In the one play the treatment is farcical, in the other it begins in tragedy and ends in miracle, and it seems that this theme of death and rebirth, and the dramatic structures through which they might be expressed, may have been developing in Shakespeare's imagination for a very long time before he turned his energies to the form of the other-worldly romances.

A second ancient Greek city was home to two Shakespearean dramas as deeply contrasting as it is possible to imagine: Athens is the setting of *Timon of Athens*, grim, desolate in its in view of humanity, and distinguished as probably his least popular play, and *A Midsummer Night's Dream*, poetic, playful and decidedly among the three or four best-loved plays of all. Athens was obviously a city that had played a unique part in the history

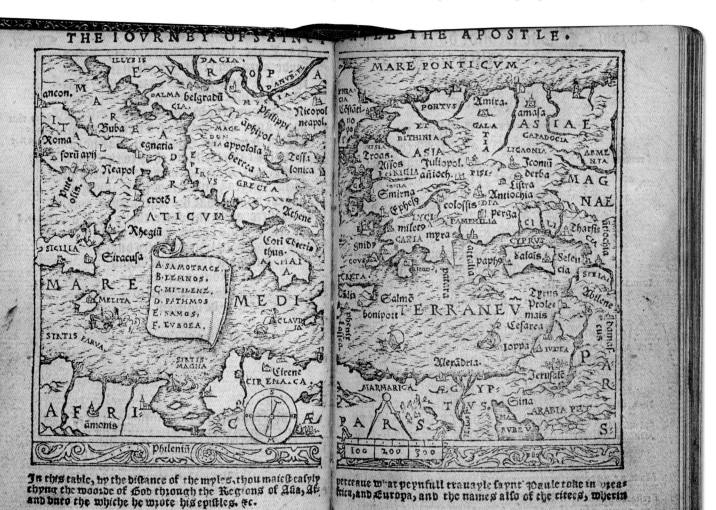

THE IOVRNEY OF SAINCT PAVLE THE APOSTLE.

In this table, by the distance of the myles, thou maist easyly chyng the woorde of God through the Regions of Asia, Affa and vnto the whiche he wrote his epistles, &c.

perceaue what peynfull trauayle saynct Paule toke in Asia, Affrica, and Europa, and the names also of the citees, wherin of civilization, but as a place it had by Shakespeare's time been unknown and unvisited by western Europeans for centuries, and neither he nor his audience can have formed any clear image of it, save that it was great and noble in rather the same way that Rome was. In Roman times Athens had been still an important city and capital of the Roman province of Achaea. It remained a centre of classical learning, and for many generations the Christian Church found it difficult to get a firm foothold there. Its eventual Christianization was inevitable, however, and Athens's decline is thought to date from 529 CE when the Emperor Justinian finally closed the pagan schools, supposedly because they were still under the sway of determined pagans. Athens's partial physical destruction at the hands of invading Slavs followed not many years later. Political and economic power shifted decisively to Constantinople, and Athens became a relatively unimportant place. The Parthenon and other temples became Christian churches, until they were transformed into mosques following the Turkish capture of the city in 1458, just five years after the fall of Constantinople itself; the Parthenon bell tower, erected by the Christians, became a minaret. This is how John Speed, the Jacobean geographer and map-maker, lamented the fate of post-classical Greece:

> Greece was once the seat of the world's empire, and flourished
> far beyond all other kind in every kind of humane learning. ...
> But the inhabitants are now curbed and kept low in knowledge
> as in estate by the tyranny of the Turks ... they are fallen from
> the noble disposition of their predecessors and become the most
> miserable objects of pity living upon the earth.[1]

It is little wonder that western visitors to Athens were few. Had Athens lain directly on the route to the Holy Land, perhaps pilgrim travellers might have visited there, and scholars too, interested in seeing the city of the great Aristotle, whose systems of logic, metaphysics and science dominated the medieval universities – Plato (and the Greek dramatists and historians) being then virtually unread. But this did not happen, and throughout the sixteenth and seventeenth centuries few travellers cared to explore Athens, so images of the city and knowledge of its appearance and setting are both non-existent. Troy, its war and its fall, meant a great deal

to all literate people, and even perhaps to many who were semi-literate. But Athens was a place of intellectual history and of a literature known to few in sixteenth-century England. It is unlikely, for example, that Shakespeare had any knowledge at all of Greek drama, except possibly through Roman imitations such as those by Seneca. Athens was therefore an ancient place of legend and hearsay only, not one easily visualized in any specific way. By 1510, Raphael, it is true, had painted in the Vatican his beautiful, evocative *School of Athens*, but this was an interior, and a work of imagination, not of topographical evocation, and it was in any case unknown in England in the sixteenth century.

Raphael's designs for tapestries illustrating the Book of Acts, commissioned by Pope Julius II, are more relevant for three reasons. First, the series includes the specifically open-air scene representing part of the ancient city, the episode of Paul's preaching on Mars Hill, where the Temple of Mars and other buildings are shown in a recognizable classical style, although an incidental portrait of Pope Julius listening to the Apostle rather undermines any claim to authenticity. Second, these designs were used again for another

17 Athens as it would have appeared to a sixteenth- or seventeenth-century visitor, with the fortified walls around the Acropolis built and rebuilt by Romans, Christians and Turks. From Stuart and Revett, *Antiquities of Athens*, 1762.

set of tapestries, produced for King Henry VIII, which were hung in the Royal Collection, although they no longer exist. Third, the designs were copied and published in engraved form during the sixteenth century, so it is at least possible that Shakespeare and some of his contemporaries would have been aware of this image of Athens as a classical city, although not of the most famous features on the Acropolis. It is fascinating to recall that the buildings on the Acropolis had remained relatively unscathed until 1687, when a Venetian bombardment of the Turkish garrison there inflicted severe damage on the Parthenon roof. Crude prints of this event, the first images of modern Athens, did begin to appear in Europe in the 1690s, showing also that the Acropolis was walled as a fortress, and we now know that it had been so since Roman times.

Only with the revolution of taste in the eighteenth century, and the revival of classical models, did western visitors turn their attention to Athens, and they began to bring back drawings showing the contemporary appearance of the city. Among these were the important English series by Stuart and Revett, published from 1762 onwards as *Antiquities of*

18 St Paul preaching on Mars Hill in Athens, a Renaissance image of the city by Raphael, used as the basis for the series of great tapestries for the Vatican, with copies elsewhere, including Hampton Court; engraved by Nicolas Dorigny in *Pinacotheca Hamptoniana*, 1719.

19 Alcibiades, the great Athenian soldier who plays an enigmatic role in *Timon*; drawing by Veneziano, *c.*1530.

Athens. The images were elegantly engraved, and showed the many famous structures, partly ruined perhaps but still noble, and purer in spirit than Roman buildings. They also showed groups of the picturesque modern inhabitants in Turkish costume, and it may be fair to assume that Athens and its people would have looked in Shakespeare's day much as they looked to Stuart and Revett – except for the unfortunate Parthenon. There are no specific locations mentioned in *Timon* and the action takes place in private houses, so the Athenian setting would be indicated by costume and interior detail. The woods to which Timon exiles himself in the second half of the play might be the woods of England.

By a strange coincidence, the other Athenian play is also divided between private interiors and woodlands, and with *A Midsummer Night's Dream* too there is an absence of any very specific sense of place. *Timon*, the story of a man's descent into savage misanthropy, was a morality tale as ancient as *Pericles*; it was to be found in the work of two Greek authors, Plutarch and Lucian, and was later retold by many Renaissance writers. But the *Dream* has no such specific source. The overriding impression that we take from the *Dream* is of the woodlands haunted by fairies, by bewitched lovers and a band of rough working men trying to be actors; so we have the puzzle of why this play should be set in Athens.

The only possible clue lies in the play's framework, in the person of Theseus, and his approaching marriage to Hippolyta. This element of the story Shakespeare took over directly from Chaucer, who used it as the opening of 'The Knight's Tale' in *The Canterbury Tales*, and from the same tale he also borrowed the idea of the two men in love with the same woman. Theseus was the national hero of Athens, who had supposedly united Attica, and about whom many legends were told, including his war against the Amazon women, when he won their queen, Hippolyta, to be his bride. He was always one of the best-known figures from antiquity, a

20 The Turkish inhabitants of Athens as a visitor of Shakespeare's time would have seen them; from Stuart and Revett, *Antiquities of Athens*, 1762.

21 Map of Oxfordshire from Drayton's *Poly-Olbion*, 1612. Drayton's England was inhabited exclusively by goddesses, nymphs and fairies of hill, wood and stream, and these maps are perhaps the nearest thing we have to a visualization of *A Midsummer Night's Dream*.

military hero, a law giver, but a fallible man of passion, and later the victim of tragedy through his faithless wife Phaedra. The dramatic possibilities of untying the lovers' confusion immediately before a wedding celebration, and of performing the play within a play which closes the drama, made it natural to retain Theseus and his marriage, and therefore the Athenian setting, in spite of the wholly rural English feel of the woodland and its fairies. The blend of fantasy and marriage celebrations has prompted many

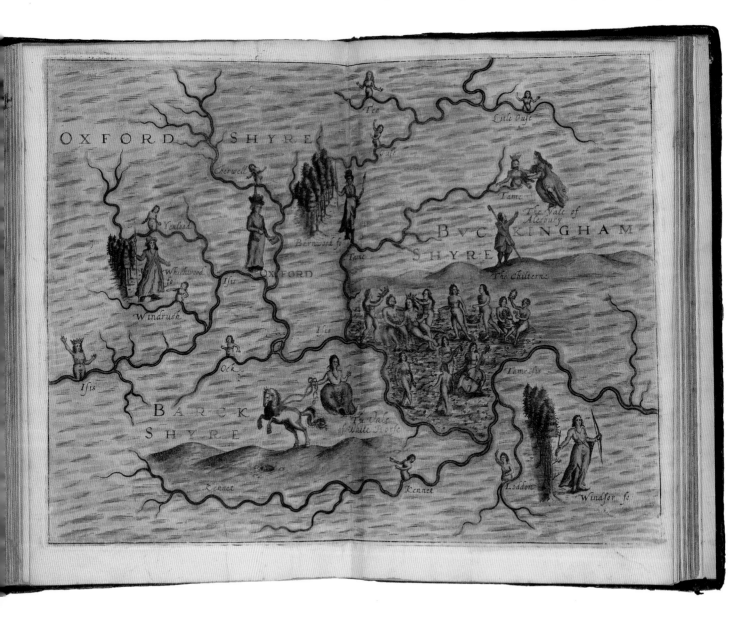

commentators to suggest that the play could have been written for the occasion of some private nuptials, before its transfer to stage and to print, but this attractive theory has never been substantiated. How much Shakespeare knew about Greek literature and culture, even from translated works, is uncertain, but the fact is that little of the reality of classical Athens enters into either play, not surprisingly since that reality was all but unknown. This was emphatically not the case with Rome.

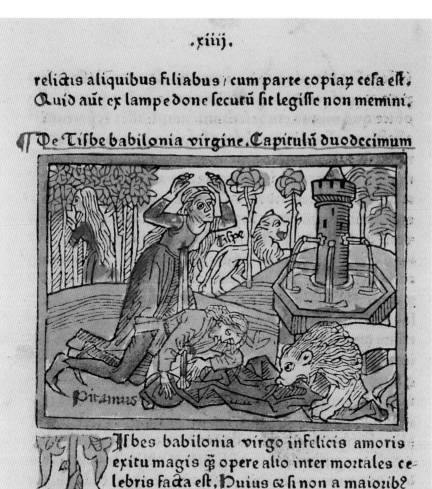

.xiiij.

relictis aliquibus filiabus / cum parte copiaꝝ cesa est.
Quid aut ex lampe done secutū sit legisse non memini.

¶ De Tisbe babilonia virgine. Capitulū duodecimum

Tisbes babilonia virgo infelicis amoris
exitu magis g̃ opere alio inter mortales ce-
lebris facta est. Huius & si non a maioribꝰ
nn̄is qui parentes fuerint haburimꝰ / intra
tn̄ babiloniam habuisse cum piramo etatis sue puero
contiguas domos satis creditum é. Quoꝝ cū esset iure
conuicinij / quasi conuictus assiduus / & inde eis adhuc
pueris puerilis affectio egit iniqua sors vt crescentibꝰ
annis(cum ambo formosissimi essent)puerilis amor in
maximum augeretur incendium / illudꝗ inter se nutibꝰ
saltem apirent aliqn̄ / iam in puberem ꝑpinquantes
etatem. Sane cum iam grandiuscula fieret tisbes a pa

22 'A tedious brief scene of young Pyramus and his love Thisbe', from an illustrated edition of Boccaccio's *De Mulieribus Claris*, 1473.

ARTHA

GOLFO DEL ARTHA

S. GEORGIO

BASTIA

S. NICOLO

RIGNASSA

PORTO FANARO

VATHI

PREVESSA

VONISA

TENPIO D'APOLLINE

SENO

AMBRACIO

S. MAVRA

The Roman plays

THE IDEA OF Rome had never ceased to dominate the European intellect and imagination, for the city had made the unique transition from being the world's dominant secular power to being its dominant spiritual power. In doing so it had retained from the imperial age the language, the historical roots, the psychology and the self-conscious grandeur of the city of the Caesars. After much hesitation, the early Christian Church decided to accept a great deal of the legacy of the past, which was of course a pagan past, but which it realized was intimately bound up with the new order. The inheritance of Roman language, literature and learning, much of it having been absorbed from Greece, was to be retained, to be valid subjects of study. Behind all this, the very idea of a universal empire remained, transposed to the spiritual realm and embodied in the structures of the universal Church. The effect of this transition was that Rome did not die: it was not destroyed in the barbarian invasions of the fifth century; it remained absolutely central to European politics, thought and culture, a fact made explicit by the coronation of Charlemagne in the year 800 as the new Holy Roman Emperor. The history, the civilization, the power, the personalities of ancient Rome were seen as forming the rock from which European history had been hewn, and as such bequeathing ideals and values which were permanent, a source of inspiration which would never be exhausted.

The crucial thing about those ideals and values was that they were secular, they were pre-Christian, they reached back into an age when belief

23 The naval Battle of Preveza, 1538, between Venetians and Turks, which took place in exactly the same waters as the Battle of Actium; only the cannon fire reveals that this is a sixteenth-century battle.

and conduct were guided by more elemental human forces; in a word, they were pagan. The Roman legacy permitted a kind of alternative value system to survive for a thousand years and more, alongside orthodox Christian norms. Rome and narratives of its history became the focus or the vehicle for displaying the masculine, martial qualities of pride, both personal and national, courage, dignity, self-discipline and self-sacrifice. But alongside this overarching self-belief, a sense that the world was their world, there was also a fatalistic acceptance that failure and defeat were always possible, that the gods or blind fate might snatch away all that the individual builds up, and that in this case those same qualities should dictate that he must meet his end calmly, turning even death into a form of victory; thus they maintained the special glory and grandeur of the fact of being Roman. Roman literature was steeped in these ideals, as were the Roman biographical studies by the Greek author Plutarch, which Shakespeare knew intimately in the English translation by Sir Thomas North of 1579, and used as the basis of his Roman plays – except *Titus Andronicus*, which is invented. The power and validity of these ideals were proved by Rome's

24 The assassination of Julius Caesar, *cassone* painting by Apollonia and Giamberti, *c*.1470.

rise to the status of world-conqueror, a role for which Elizabethan England, since the triumphs of Francis Drake and the humiliation of the Armada, seemed to be already preparing itself.

Rome the city never declined into obscurity the way that Athens did, for it was known and visited throughout the post-classical era, but its fabric suffered destruction, neglect and rebuilding, obscuring the legacy of the pagan past. With the departure of Constantine to his new eastern capital, the Bishop of Rome assumed effective temporal power over the city, and the basilica of St Peter's formed the new urban focus. For all its symbolic importance, Rome contracted physically, to a population estimated at 20,000 to 30,000 from an estimated 1 million at its height in the first century CE. Large areas of the ancient city were gardens, pastures, vineyards or wasteland. Armed conflicts between the popes and the medieval commune led to further destruction, and the period of the Avignon Papacy brought still more desolation; around 1400 Rome was described as a city of thieves, vermin and decay, where wolves roamed at night.

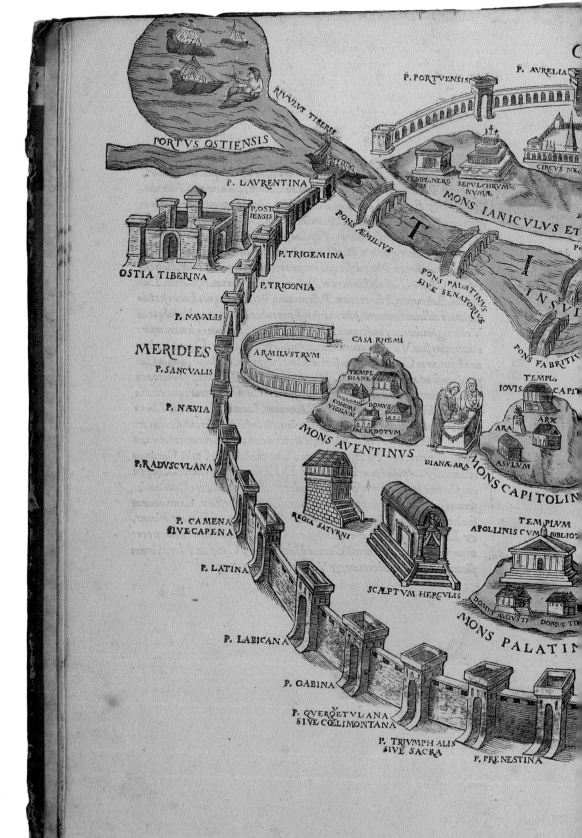

25 A diagrammatic map of Rome at the time of Augustus, divided into sixteen districts corresponding to the sixteen gates, each with a major structure – temple, baths, arch, circus, column or tomb. From Calvo's *Antiquae Urbis Romae*, 1556.

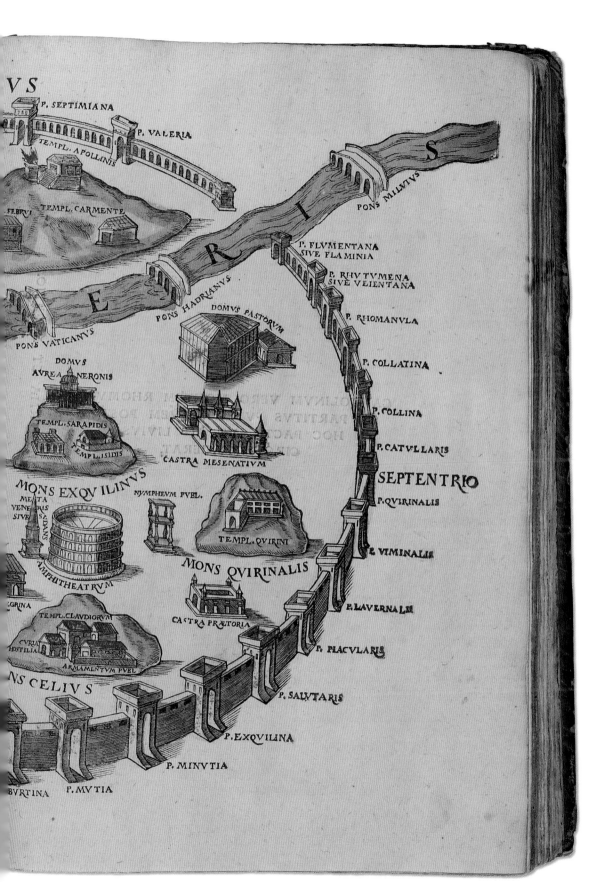

VS
P. SEPTIMIANA
P. VALERIA
TEMPL. APOLLINIS
TEMPL. CARMENTE
FEBRIS
PONS VATICANVS
PONS HADRIANVS
DOMVS PASTORVM
DOMVS
AVREA NERONIS
TEMPL. SARAPIDIS
TEMPL. ISIDIS
CASTRA MESENATIVM
MONS EXQVILINVS
META
VENERIS
SIVE ADANS
NYMPHEVM PVBL.
TEMPL. QVIRINI
MONS QVIRINALIS
AMPHITHEATRVM
PEREGRINA
TEMPL. CLAVDIORVM
CASTRA PRÆTORIA
CVRIA
HOSTILIA
ARMAMENTVM PVBL.
NS CELIVS
BVRTINA
P. MVTIA
P. MINVTIA
P. EXQVILINA
P. SALVTARIS
P. PIACVLARIS
P. LAVERNALIS
P. VIMINALIS
P. QVIRINALIS
SEPTENTRIO
P. CATVLLARIS
P. COLLINA
P. COLLATINA
P. RHOMANVLA
P. RHVTVMENA
SIVE VEIENTANA
P. FLVMENTANA
SIVE FLAMINIA
PONS MILVIVS
S
R
I
E
B

The end of the papal schism in *c.*1420 and the entry of Pope Martin V into Rome were the precondition for a revival. Rome entered a period of almost two centuries during which lessons were learned from the renaissance of art in Florence and the return to classical models. A succession of popes, seeing themselves paradoxically as Renaissance humanists and princes, undertook the task of clearing the slums and rebuilding the city, a process in which the recovery of ancient glories was the aim, and the study of ancient structures and carvings was vitally important. The celebrated sculpture Laocoön, one of the supreme examples of classical art, was discovered in a vineyard in 1506 and installed in the Vatican, and the Apollo Belvedere followed soon afterwards. There was huge interest among scholars, artists and their patrons in what the classical city had looked like, and books of engravings were published, some showing the antiquities, others the new buildings of the sixteenth century. In 1579, Stefano du Perac published his great map that claimed to show the ancient city in its entirety. His map was a wonderful work of art, showing the buildings in elevation, but inevitably involved some inaccuracies and a good deal of guesswork.

Historic events from ancient Rome, such as the assassination of Julius Caesar, came to be seen as fit subjects for artists, while the genre of the

triumph became especially popular. Andrea Mantegna painted a series of *Triumphs of Caesar* for the Gonzaga family, a powerful testimony to the growing cult of antiquity. Similar scenes reached the public in the form of engravings, and showed Roman power at its most visually exciting: trophies and prisoners taken in foreign wars paraded through the streets, in scenes inspired by, if not actually copied from, Trajan's column, the Arch of Constantine, and other storiated monuments. Extant statues and reliefs showed Roman dress, Roman armour and Roman soldiers in combat. There is no question that Rome had a strong visual identity for the people of Shakespeare's age, and we know from the earliest illustrations of plays in production that the Roman plays were always enriched by Roman costume, whereas the other plays showed a distinct lack of any historical sense in their use of costume.

All the Roman plays both assume and question the classical Roman martial qualities. *Titus Andronicus* is not an authentic Roman story and is a special case, being an invented, bloodthirsty revenge tragedy, set in the last days of the Empire in the shadow of the barbarian attacks. Yet even here in the first of the Roman plays, endurance and fortitude are central as Titus and his family are martyred one by one with barbaric

26 A Roman triumph in which defeated kings and generals were led in chains through the streets of Rome, exactly as in the opening of *Titus Andronicus*. Decorative panels added to Perac's map of Rome, 1570.

cruelty. But Titus' fortitude finally cracks, and he embarks on his course of demonic revenge, implicitly discarding the Roman code of honour and meeting his own death, leaving the stage bathed in blood. In *Julius Caesar* the issue is simpler: Caesar has carried his Roman sense of pride and power so far that his political ambition threatens the common good; he appears to be crossing the line dividing men from gods, or so his enemies believe. Brutus is Caesar's opposite, who must reassert the ideal of selfless duty by killing him, risking his own life in the process for the greater good of Rome, and earning the epitaph of 'the noblest Roman of them all'.[2] Coriolanus too represents aristocratic Roman pride, in his case joined with absolute disdain for physical danger. Outmanoeuvred by his enemies, he conceives a bitter hatred for the city to which he was once devoted, and makes war on Rome. Only the impassioned pleading of his family diverts his anger, but this submission to softer human feeling means that he in turn will be killed by his own forces. In *Antony and Cleopatra* we again, and still more clearly, see the conflict between the forces of honour and pride, and those of emotion. The play is symmetrically divided

27 Philomela raped and mutilated by Tereus, the story from Ovid which provided some of the plot for *Titus Andronicus*; from a German edition of 1569.

between Rome and Alexandria, between duty and pleasure, and it is Antony who vacillates between the two, compromising his integrity and reputation as a soldier, and finally throwing away honour and life for human love; yet even at the very end salvaging his pride through suicide, 'a Roman by a Roman / Valiantly vanquish'd'.[3] Alexandria is pictured as a place of irresponsibility and oriental hedonism, the capital of a nation and a dynasty with no future. Rome as a place of coldness, severity and discipline, qualities which however give them mastery over the world. The contrast between the two settings, the two geographical locations, has a cumulative psychological effect that underlines the dramatic theme of the play. Antony's opening lines dismissing Rome and all that it stands for announce that theme with great force and clarity: 'Let Rome in Tiber melt, and the wide arch / Of the rang'd empire fall!'[4]

Antony and Cleopatra possesses also the added interest of the other locations in the play around the eastern Mediterranean where Antony's armies meet those of Octavius, above all at the Battle of Actium, fought off the west coast of mainland Greece. That region would have been largely unknown to anyone in Shakespeare's England, but as it happens a much

28 Ovid again: Tereus tricked into eating the flesh of his murdered children, again directly paralleled in *Titus.*

29 (*overleaf*) The city and harbour of Alexandria in 1572; here an Islamic city dominated by its mosques, the Roman remains are still in evidence. From Braun and Hogenberg's *Civitates Orbis Terrarum*, 1572.

ALEXA

Porta Nili.

S Cath

Porte du Cairo

Sub hoc lapide
Corpus S Marci
nium, et ...
Venetia ...
cath

Baßar

MOSQVE

...lua palmarum, ad usum
...nium, et medulla, quæ
...r urbe venalis est.

Obeliscus

Domus

Pharus

Guardia

30 Coriolanus struggling with
the pleas of his wife and mother
to spare Rome; engraving after a
painting by Poussin, 1650.

more recent sea battle had been fought in exactly the same waters, off
Preveza at the mouth of what was by then named the Gulf of Arta, where
in 1538 a Christian fleet was defeated by a Turkish fleet. Engravings of the
Battle of Preveza (ultimately less famous than the later Battle of Lepanto,
where the outcome was reversed) were published in Italy. If we ignore the
cannon smoke seen rising from the ships, these pictures could easily be
taken as showing the Battle of Actium, 1,500 years earlier, for the galleys
used on both sides were recognizably the direct descendants of the Roman
galley.

   In the Roman plays, an equally famous location outside of Rome itself
is Philippi, close to the northern shores of the Aegean, where, in *Julius
Caesar*, Octavius and Antony meet and destroy the army of Caesar's
assassins, Brutus and Cassius. The name Philippi is very familiar from the
scene in which Caesar's ghost visits Brutus, warning him, 'Thou shalt see
me at Philippi'.5 *Coriolanus* presents the somewhat recherché problem of
who exactly the Volscians were. A region of that name was shown on the

Ptolemaic maps, north and east of Rome, and its people are mentioned by Roman historians as enemies in the early phase of Roman history. By around 300 BCE, however, they had been subdued and absorbed into the Latin world. Of the city of Corioli itself there is no known trace, but the name Monti Volsini survives near Orvieto.

In Shakespearean tragedy, forces of conflict and disorder are let loose in the lives of the principal characters, and cannot be healed, only ended in death. The pagan Roman background, with its stern code of courage, fortitude and stoical resignation, made an ideal setting for exploring the cost of obedience to this harsh code in the lives of individual men and women. They test the limits to which men will be driven by national or political loyalties. There is no reference anywhere to spiritual beliefs or imperatives, for these are purely secular dramas about the worldly glory, the worldly power and the price that they extract from those who gain them. In these plays the specific topography of Rome is rarely of any great importance, though the Forum and the Capitol are mentioned; it is the city as a symbol of power that is important, the city bestowing fame and honour, but devouring people as it makes history. Not only Rome's external enemies, but those Romans who struggle to resist or throw off its code of obedience, are destroyed, such is the all-consuming power of the idea of Rome.

31 A Roman army marching with the emperor, one of a series of reliefs by Giulio Romano, *c.*1530, engraved by Bartoli in 1680.

The
Mediterranean plays

TROY, ATHENS, EPHESUS, the coasts of Syria, the Aegean, Rome and Alexandria: the common factor, the great geographical link between them, is the Mediterranean Sea. It has always been recognized that without the Mediterranean the history and culture of Europe could not have developed in the way that they did, forming a superhighway linking so many nations. Dr Johnson, speaking in his usual oracular manner, expressed this perfectly:

> Sir, a man who has not been in Italy is always conscious of an
> inferiority from his not having seen what it is expected a man
> should see. The grand object of travelling is to see the shores of
> the Mediterranean. On those shores were the four great empires
> of the world: the Assyrian, the Persian, the Greek and the
> Roman. All our religion, almost all our law, almost all our arts,
> almost all that sets us above savages, has come to us from the
> shores of the Mediterranean.[6]

The crucial point about the Mediterranean is that this great inland sea did not divide peoples but linked them, and its ports and cities became places of ceaseless encounter and exchange, not of commodities alone, but of ideas and cultures.

From history and literature the immense importance of the Mediterranean was perfectly familiar as the setting of Greek and Roman civilization. The supreme works of Greek and Latin literature, *The Odyssey* and *The Aeneid*, both have Mediterranean voyages as their central episodes. Greek

32 Piazza San Marco from Braun and Hogenberg; this might almost be a scene from a Venetian play like *The Merchant of Venice* or *Othello*.

legends like that of Jason and the Argonauts were founded on the premiss that there were fabled lands and peoples effectively on the other side of world, to which no Greek had ever sailed before. To the Greeks, the Mediterranean was *Mesogeios*, 'the midst of the earth', and to the Romans it was *mare internum*, 'the internal sea', effectively a vast lake sitting at the heart of the Empire. The Christian Church as a power in the world came into being when St Paul left its Palestinian homeland and crossed the Mediterranean to take his message to Asia – that is, modern Turkey – to Greece and to Rome. For the Crusaders and for generations of pilgrims, the commonest route to the Holy Land was overland to Venice, and thence by sea to one of the ports such as Acre or Joppa. Venice was the great commercial contact point between western Europe and the Byzantine Empire.

The decisive event which impacted on the nations bordering the Mediterranean was the rise of Islam. Between 640 and 700 CE, Muslim armies erupted from Arabia and drove westward through Egypt along the entire North African coastline to Tangier. Crossing the Straits of Gibraltar, they overran Spain, before being turned back in the heart of France. At the same time other forces had taken Syria, from where naval campaigns were mounted against Cyprus and Rhodes; while Crete, Sicily, Sardinia and Corsica fell in the ninth century. The Mediterranean was emphatically no longer a Roman lake or a Christian lake, for the larger part of it was shared

33 Cyprus and the eastern Mediterranean, from Rosaccio's *Viaggio da Venetia a Costantinopoli*, 1598. No place names on the island are mentioned in *Othello*; all the action seems to take place in a port rather than an inland city such as Nicosia.

pour auoir des oracles et reuelatiõs, ou Alexãdre eut reuelation qu'il feroit dominateur de tout le mõde: toutesfois qu'il ne retourneroit point en vie en fon pays:ce qui aduint. Car en retournãt en Macedoine il fuft empoifõne en la ville de Babylon, ou il mourut.

De l'Indie qui eft outre la

riuiere de Ganges.

Ombien que cefte Indie foit merueilleufe/ment fertile & bien cultiuée, toutesfois on trouue en icelle aufsi bien qu'en la premiere beaucoup de defertz, plufieurs & diuers hommes & beftes fauuages, & ce à caufe de la grand chaleur qu'ilz ont. Pline recite des habitans de cefte terre, qu'ilz font tellemẽt halez de l'ardeur du foleil qu'ilz en deuiennẽt noirs, cõme font aufsi les Ethiopiens: non pas que la chaleur du foleil face feulemẽt cela, mais la femẽce

noire de ces hõmes les fait premierement noirs, & puis l'ardeur du foleil y adioufte de la couleur d'auantage. Les anciens ont forgé beaucoup de fortes de monftres, lefquelz on trouue en cefte region, comme ilz affirment. Entre autres Solin et Megaftenes difent qu'en diuerfes montagnes d'Indie il y a des gẽs qui ont la tefte cõme vn chien, & abbayent comme les chiẽs, fans pouoir former aucune parolle humaine, & pour tous vetemens ont des brayes qui leur couurent les feffes & les parties honteufes. Ceux qui habitent pres de la fource de Ganges, n'ont nul befoing d'ayde pour viure: car ilz viuent de l'odeur des pommes fauuages. Que s'il aduient qu'ilz ayent attiré à eux quelque puante & mauuaife haleine, il eft certain qu'ilz en meurent: & on dit qu'ils'en eft trouué

34 'The anthropophagi, and men whose heads / Do grow beneath their shoulders' seen by Othello. The ancient belief in half-human creatures dwelling outside the civilized world was still widespread among Renaissance geographers. From Münster's *Cosmographia*, 1552.

with, if not actually controlled by, the forces of Islam. In addition to the official fleets of the various Islamic powers there was the threat of piracy, as along the North African and Syrian coasts, from Tangier to Antioch, whole communities lived on plunder and the trade in prisoners through the slave markets, a situation which persisted for centuries. The North African shore was called the 'Barbary Coast', derived from the word Berber, but carrying the inevitable association of 'barbarism'.

After the fall of Constantinople in 1453, the nation which confronted Turkish sea power and pirates more than any other was Venice. The Battle of Lepanto was heralded as a triumph against Muslim aggression, and was the subject of several major paintings by Venetian artists, but its practical impact may have been largely as a morale-booster for Europeans. The dangers of sea travel in the region were vividly portrayed in several personal narratives, such as that by Edward Webbe, who was captured at sea off Tunis and forced to endure Turkish brutality as a galley slave for fifteen years before being ransomed and returned home to write his memoirs. For this reason, in the age of Shakespeare direct English experience of the Mediterranean was minimal, but as a place made famous by history and legend its resonance was undiminished.

The presence of Islamic and then of Turkish power coloured the entire European perception of what Asia – that is, Turkey and the lands of the eastern Mediterranean generally – meant. John Speed published the first English world atlas in 1627, the maps interspersed with geographical descriptions and comments. Here he speaks of the past glories of Asia, as the region where 'God spoke in the miraculous work of creation'; where 'the first peoples of the world received their being'; home of the first kings, the first languages; it was 'blessed by God's holy presence'; the saviour of the world was born there; it was rich and plentiful in all things. But now, Speed warns, Asia is punished for its infidelities; it is delivered 'into the hands of Turks and nations that blaspheme their creator'; it is inhabited by wild beasts, so that men live there 'not without much danger', and even men are found there who have 'such monstrous shapes as pass belief'.[7] This was the alien, unchristian world which the European imagination saw on its eastern frontiers.

As well as the plays set in the ancient world – *Pericles*, *The Comedy of Errors* and *Antony and Cleopatra* – three Shakespeare plays and one by Marlowe have a Mediterranean background. *Othello* is a play rich in geographical allusions, but few of them are clear-cut. From its Venetian opening, the action shifts in act 2 to Cyprus, where Othello has been sent to command the Venetian fleet against the approaching Turks. The enemy, however, is scattered by a storm, and the rest of the play takes place on the island, presumably either in the western port of Paphos or in Famagusta on the eastern side. No more is heard of the Turks, but the loathing felt against them by all Venetians, and presumably by all Christians, is encapsulated in Othello's dying phrases, 'a malignant and a turban'd Turk,'[8] and 'the circumcised dog'.[9] The geographical, cultural and racial undercurrents of the play are complicated by the shadow of the Turks, but still more by the Moor himself. Since the term 'moor' is imprecise in its meaning, what

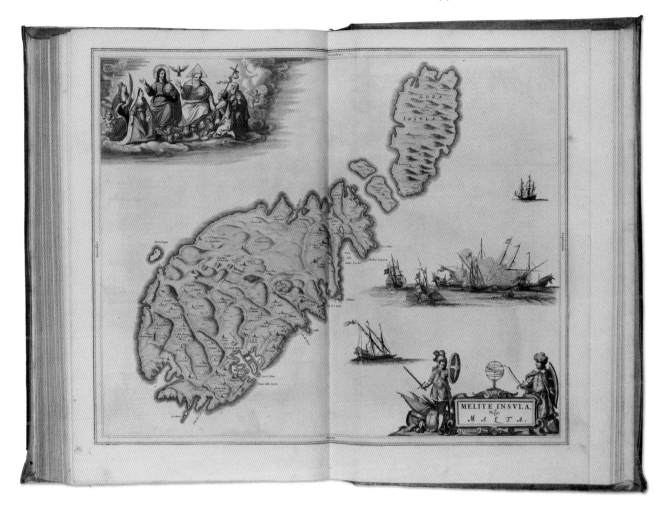

nationality should we take Othello to be? Was he North African – Egyptian or Berber in origin – or was he a sub-Saharan African?

There are difficulties with both possibilities, which years of scholarly argument have failed to settle, and we can only assume that Shakespeare and his contemporaries used the term loosely. If Othello were a Berber or an Egyptian, he would surely be a Muslim, and how could such a man be a Venetian commander against the Turks? He might conceivably be a Christian convert, but the text does not say so. Sub-Saharan Africans were known in Europe almost exclusively as slaves, and again the likelihood of one reaching high military rank in Venice or anywhere else was utterly remote. It is true that Venetian men were widely regarded as decadent worldlings, spoilt by wealth and luxury; an Elizabethan tourist, Fynes

35 The defeat of the besieging Turks by the Knights of Malta in 1565 was an event celebrated throughout Europe. In Marlowe's *The Jew of Malta* the power struggle between Christians and Turks forms the setting, with the scheming Jew making a third force; the two main parties are clearly represented on this map by Blaeu, 1660.

Moryson, says they were 'trained up in pleasure and wantonness, which must needs abase and effeminate their minds'.[10] This incidentally is why, in his opinion, Venice often turned to foreigners to command its military forces, demonstrating again that Othello, although of an alien race, was accepted as in some ways a superior being; he was the 'noble Moor', but exactly what this meant we still do not know.

The most curious historical fact about the sixteenth-century Mediterranean is this: that as the western European powers were turning their attention to the Atlantic as the gateway to world domination, their own backyard was being invaded by both land and sea by an intensely hostile power – the Turks. Some contemporaries perceived this, and pleaded for an end to internecine wars in France, the Netherlands and Italy, and for Europe to direct its energies into resisting the Turks. The Turkish presence was a source of fear and hatred, for the Turks were ruthless and non-Christian, and they were driven by a fierce desire for conquest; not surprisingly they were perceived as alien and threatening. Yet the Turkish Empire was wealthy and thriving, and in many ways was an open society, for the lure of trade followed the passion for conquest. Although resented and hated by Europeans, the Turks did not habitually bar or persecute visitors from the west. Aleppo itself, mentioned by Othello, was described in 1583 by one Elizabethan visitor, John Eldred, as 'The greatest place of traffike for a dry towne that is in all these parts: for hither resort Jewes, Tartarians, Persians, Armenians, Egyptians, Indians, and many sorts of Christians, and injoy freedome of their consciences, and bring hither many kindes of rich merchandise.'[11]

In the main source for *Othello*, a story by the Italian author Cinthio, the whole of the action takes place in Venice; therefore Shakespeare may have had some specific purpose in shifting the scene away to Cyprus, such alterations of setting being unusual with him. We use the phrase 'shifting the scene' rather lightly, perhaps forgetting that this entailed a voyage of well over a thousand miles, in effect taking the action out of the glorious city and into a foreign warzone. But the Turkish force melts away and the expected naval battle does not take place; instead a personal battle erupts in Othello's life and mind. From being 'the noble Moor', he becomes 'a black devil'. It is Othello who becomes alien, a savage fanatic, prepared to kill in his beliefs or his passions. This was exactly the conventional image of the Turk, but it also echoes the more ancient traditions concerning Cyprus: the great sixteenth-century geographer Ortelius tells us that 'The people generally do give themselves to pleasures, sports and voluptuousness ... the lasciviousness of the nation is such that vulgarly it was supposed to have been dedicated to Venus, the Goddesse of love.'[12] Thus love and war, two of the greatest forces in human history, are both concentrated on Cyprus.

Was this Shakespeare's reason for moving the drama to Cyprus, into the realm of the passionate, irrational, alien Turkish culture? Was he delineating Othello's descent into savagery, which was always there beneath the surface of his personality? We cannot be sure, but it is a possible reading, and at the very least it seems that, as in *Antony and Cleopatra*, resonances of place and culture are being exploited, and the audience is invited to witness a conflict in which the individual is morally transformed and corrupted. Watching the play around the year 1604, the audience would also have been aware that Cyprus had fallen to the Turks thirty years earlier, soon after their supposedly decisive defeat at the Battle of Lepanto; so the story they were witnessing must be taking place in the world of the past, and its tragic events could be seen as a dark omen for the island's future. The dramatic ambiguities in *Othello* are amply reflected in this complex geographical setting.

Shakespeare's other Venetian play, *The Merchant of Venice*, also centres on a problem of identity, but one that is more readily understood. Shylock is also an alien, a Jew condemned, victimized and harried throughout Europe, although often tolerated even where they were officially barred, as in Elizabethan London. The culmination of centuries of persecution in Spain and Portugal ended only with the expulsion of the Jews in 1492 and 1497, after which Italy and Ottoman lands were the only homes open to the migrants. The long tradition that the age of the Messiah would be preceded by a period of calamities seemed to be about to be fulfilled, and pseudo-Messiahs did indeed appear, but ended by losing their own lives and further alienating the Christians. Ghettoization began in Venice in 1516, and soon spread to other Italian cities. Venice was a wealthy and magnificent city, but at least some of that wealth needed the support of banks and moneylenders – people like Shylock.

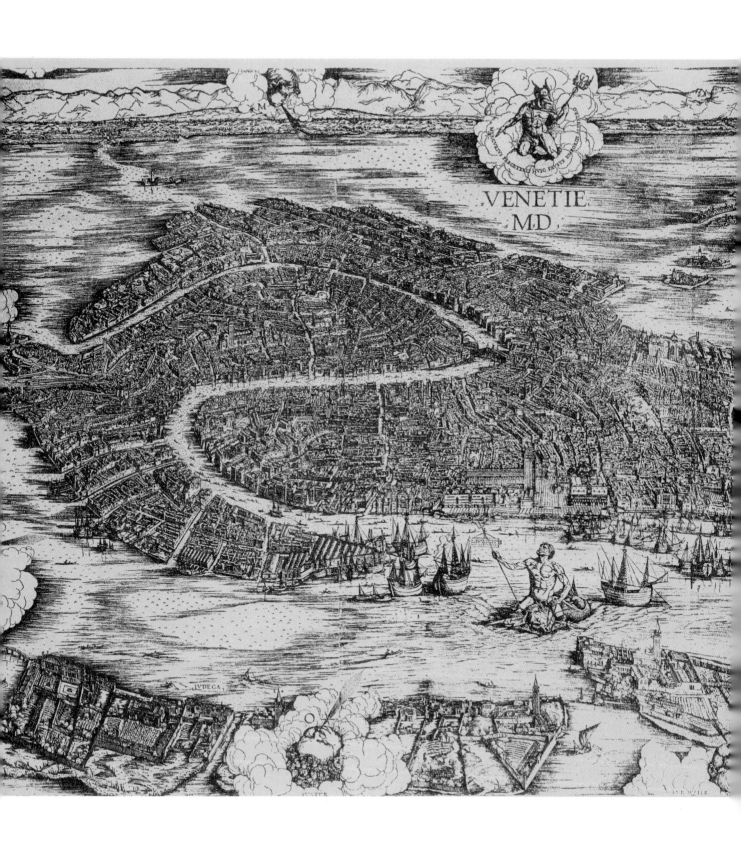

VENETIE
M.D

36 One section of the large
perspective view of Venice by
Jacopo de' Barbari printed in
1500. This work of precision and
imagination is a breathtaking
tribute to the city's unique
grandeur.

Antonio, the merchant of the play's title, has invested, some would say gambled, boldly in foreign ventures: he has fleets bound for Tripolis, for the Indies, for Mexico and for England. The list displays Venice as the centre of a vast web of maritime trade, but one that is terribly vulnerable, and the loss of these ships at sea provides Shylock with his opportunity for revenge. Shakespeare uses the centuries-old hatred between Christians and Jews to explore, as in *Othello*, the condition of being different, alien, an object of fear or hatred. The question is not whether Shakespeare, or this play, is anti-Semitic; he is not simply saying 'see what monsters these Jews are', but rather 'treat people with cruelty and they will respond with cruelty.' 'If you wrong us shall we not revenge?' Is this not a fundamental instinct, one that in fact proves Shylock all too human? As has often been noticed, the Christians in *The Merchant* are eaten up with hatred and fail to live up to the ideals of their faith, giving some justification to Shylock's actions as a natural, self-defensive response. Shylock is no caricature but a living being, proud, shrewd and passionate. Shylock's story, like Othello's, has the Venetian–Mediterranean world as its essential background, for neither story could have worked so effectively in London, Paris or Vienna. Aaron the Moor in *Titus Andronicus* is a pantomime devil in comparison with Othello, partly because in ancient Italy he appears to have no place; there is no comprehensible reason why he should be there.

Alongside *Pericles*, the second play intimately connected with the sea, with the Mediterranean, with identity and with transformation, is of course *The Tempest*. The storm and shipwreck of the King of Naples and his party occur as they are returning from Tunis to Naples. Islands are not plentiful in those waters, except for those close to Sicily, and none of them seems suitable, so the true identity of Prospero's island remains an academic quibble. For the literal-minded there is the second teasing problem of how Prospero, when he was thrown out of Milan and cast adrift in a leaky boat (presumably in the Gulf of Genoa) could have sailed so far south, beyond Naples, before finding his island. As early as the eighteenth century, scholars identified an important source in the published accounts of a shipwreck in the Bermudas in 1609, which provided very clear verbal and thematic inspiration for the play, not least the fact that the Bermudas had long been regarded by mariners as a haunt of devils or evil spirits.

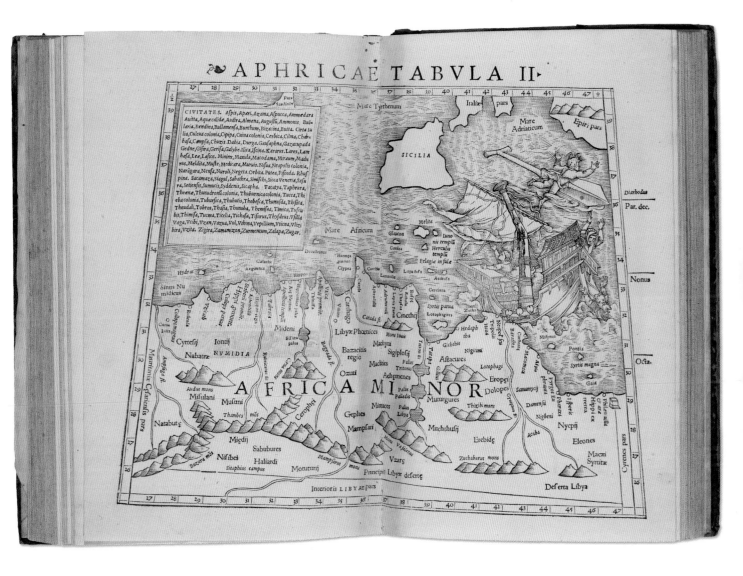

Several generations would pass, however, before any suggestion arose that *The Tempest* was somehow really about Bermuda and the New World, and was not a Mediterranean play at all. Such an interpretation only gathered real force in the twentieth century, which saw the true subject of the play as colonialism, and which elevated the figure of Caliban to a central place in it, as an emblem of slavery.

This conception of the play, although now well established, is still open to serious doubt. Most of the evidence in the text supports the common-sense view that the play has a Mediterranean setting. Caliban was not

37 A ship wrecked in a Mediterranean storm somewhere between Tunisia and Sicily, an image that provides an uncanny parallel to *The Tempest*'s opening scene; from the Münster Ptolemy Atlas of 1540.

VIRGI
R G
ori:

Ca.Henry
Roanoak

Mappa ÆSTIV.
alias BARMVD.
Mexicani æstuarij jace
duum 32 Minutorum
Scilicet versus Libe
Anglicanis, et a Ro
in Virginia) versu
accurate

Daniels Iland

SOMERSETI
INSVLA

13 Chamber
lain bay
12
14
11   15
SOMERSCET
10
ILAND
5

Flemish
wreck

Heydon

Hog bay
Sandys
2
Sandys narrow.

HIBERNIA

IRELAND

Gates
Iland
Walford
Iland

LATVM

FRETVM   Pearle
Iland

The Great Sound

Spanish point

Abbotts bay

Bermudas l

Pembroke
Tribe

Brackish

Devonf

1
16
15   14
13
South
12
11

Brother
Ilands

White heartie
52
49

Rickes Ila:

Ca. Turket Iland

Elisabeth
Iland

Agers
Il:

Dorrel Iland

Pagets   port

Pagets

48 47
46
45 44 43 42
40 39 38 37 36 35 34 33 32 31 30 29 28 27
19 18 17 16 15
6   5

amp
ton   Tribe
9
8

Warwick

Tribe

Pagets   Tribe

26 25 24 23   22 21 20
19 18 17 16 15 14 13 12   11 10 9 8 7 6 5 4 3 2 1
16 15 14 13 12 11 10 9 8 7 6 5

4
3
2

Port Royal

Great Turkle bay

Elbow bay

G L I A
England

Insularum,
m, ad Ostia
itudine Gra:
lia, Londino
Miliaribus
locus est
500 Mill.

Tobacco bay   Sandys fort
Warwick fort
Whalebone bay   ILAND
Burnt point   *Worserholm bay*   Davers fort
Prom. ad uftum   St GEORGES   Henn fort
                                                  Ila d
Cony Ila.   *The Stocks*   Cavendish fort
Bath   Lonabird Il   Pagets fort
The Staggs   Oblongarum   Smiths Ila. Smiths fort
              Hammilton 14 13 12 11 10 9 8 7 6 5 Avium Insula   St. Davids
                                                  Iland.
            Haring: Walsingham
      toni Fretum.   bay
                    3   Dav
Sounds   hea
mouth   Harington   2   SOVTHAMTONIÆ PORTVS
              Schnd   Coopers
Smiths Tribe   Tribe Part of   Southampton Harbour   Iland
                         Tuckers   Nonsuch
14 13 12 11 10 9 8 7 6 5 4 3 2 1 Towne   Kings Castle   Pem:
                      the Generall iland Stokes bay   Yoorts brook fort
                                                      land
Harriffes bay   Charles   Gurnets head Hyrcæ promont.
                                          fort

...tium Anno 1616 folvere ex his Insulis
Schapha superne aperta, trium doliorum
...atis, et post septem hebdomadarum

Scala trium Miliarum vel vigintiquatuor Stadiorum.

the ancient possessor of the island, but the offspring of a witch who was banished there from Algiers for her crimes, and he is said to have had the devil for his father. He is described not as a black slave, African or Native American, but as scaly, fishy and reptilian, and he relates more closely to the fairies, goblins and witches of *Macbeth* and *The Dream* than to any forms of oppressed humanity. English colonialism or imperialism cannot be said to have existed in Shakespeare's time, except in Ireland, and it is quite impossible that Elizabethan or Jacobean perspectives on that subject can have remotely resembled our own. It is true that in 1627 John Speed could write of divine providence being seen in 'that noble enterprise of planting Virginia with Christian religion and English people',[13] and of the role of the Bermudas as opening a passage to the New World in general and to Virginia in particular. But any idea that there was at this date even the ghost of a British Empire, with the troubling moral questions that came with it, and that this was the true subject of the play seems completely unhistorical. To see Caliban as the focal point of *The Tempest* is surely as odd as seeing Polonius as the focal point of *Hamlet*.

It is interesting to ask why neither Shakespeare nor Marlowe, although very well aware of the adventurous history of the New World, seemed interested in setting dramas there. When Marlowe wanted to depict a ruthless military conqueror fighting and slaying his way across the world's stage, he turned to the Old World, to the medieval scourge of Asia, Tamburlaine. The reason is probably this: it is true that all drama springs from conflict, but that conflict must be psychological, and it must spring from the qualities and characteristics of European man and European society. These qualities include, among others, love, honour, courage, honesty, loyalty, compassion, understanding, wisdom and humour. Such qualities could not be expressed by placing Europeans in opposition to savages, for they were all characteristics of civilization. There was also the significant fact that the nations actually then settled in the New World were Spain and Portugal only, and the record of their dealings with the native peoples was one of greed, mass cruelty and bloodshed, which were seen in Protestant England as typical of the Catholic nations. Such events would not make fit subjects for the English stage, and this alone is a strong argument against *The Tempest* having any American dimension, even a hidden one.

38 (*previous spread*) *The Tempest* was influenced by descriptions of maritime adventures in the Bermudas, but this map, copied by Blaeu from Speed's map of 1626, shows the island a few years later, neatly parcelled out among the colonists, and inconceivable as Prospero's island of spirits and magic.

The play was the last of the four late romances, in all of which personalities are tested, tried and purified by the experience of suffering, where the ordeal of sea travel and the experience of miraculous recovery are emblematic of change, transformation and self-discovery. There is even the suggestion of rebirth in the spiritual or religious sense. The all-important elements in *The Tempest*, as in *Pericles* and *The Winter's Tale*, are the obvious ones of the sea, the storm, the near-death experiences, the healing passage of time, and the reconciliation that closes these plays. This surely is the clear reason for *The Tempest's* Mediterranean setting, for the play takes the familiar theatrical ensemble of a European court and breaks it apart, dropping it down into the wilds of the sea, and the labyrinth of an enchanted island. Except for *Pericles*, no Shakespeare play shows more clearly the imaginative use of location and of geography, underlining again the force of his conception that the theatre was a globe, and that there was always 'a world elsewhere', in which the drama of his imagination could take shape.

39 The idea that Caliban is a black African or Native American is now current, but it is not supported by the text, where he is described as fishy, scaly or finny; this semi-human monster from Münster's *Cosmographia*, 1552, may be nearer to Shakespeare's intention.

Chasteau de voncennes

Picqpuce   S.t Antoine des champs

Portes S.t Antoine

La Bastille

La place
Royalle

R. S.t Antoine

P. S.t Paul

Marets du Temple

Porte du Temple   Le Temple

S.t Iean

Ville

P. de Greue

P. S.t Martin   S.t Martin   R. des Champs   P. S.t Martin   S.t Iulien

La Trinité

P. S.t Denis   le Ponseau   R.   S.t Denis

les Halles

R. Mont-orgueil

Mont-Marthe

R. Coquilliere

S.t Honoré

Porte

Faubourg montmartre   le Palmail   Marché aux Cheuaux

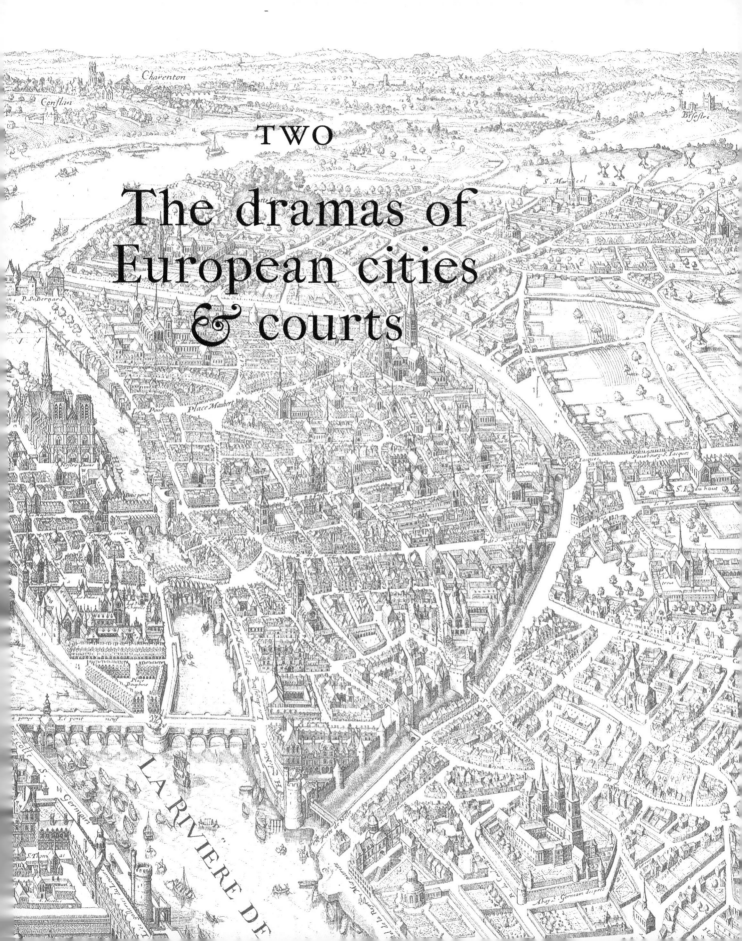

TWO
The dramas of European cities & courts

URBIUM
PRAECIPUARUM
MUNDI THEATRUM
QUINTUM
AUCTORE GEORGIO
BRAUNIO AGRIPPINATE

The idea of Europe

The nurse of the victorious, and the conquering people of all other nations of the world, most beautiful and far surpassing the rest. ... This our Europe, besides the Roman Empire reverenced of all the world, hath in all eight and twenty Christian Kingdoms, whereby you may estimate the worthiness of this region. It is a place out of all measure fruitful, and the natural disposition of his air is very temperate. For all kinds of grain, for wine, and abundance of woods, it is inferior to none, but comparable to the best of the others. It is so pleasant, and so beautified with stately cities, towns and villages, that for the courage and valour of the people and several nations, although it be less in quantity and circuit, yet might it well be accounted superior unto all other parts of the world.[1]

THESE WORDS, translated from those of the great Flemish geographer Ortelius, show us the extent to which geographical ideas in the sixteenth and seventeenth centuries were moralized. The various regions of the earth were either blessed by nature and by God, or they were frowned upon, made desolate because he had turned his back upon them and had permitted nature to show its evil aspect. In the case of Europe, it is the power of Christianity that has made her the 'tamer and subduer' of the whole world, the champion of civilization, 'as far as the fury and force of our cruel enemies will permit'. The European nations have added to their possessions the new land of America, and the richest and chiefest parts of Africa and Asia. The example of the Roman Empire is still alive in Europe's Christian princes: 'Let then the other parts of the

40 The personified and richly clothed figure of Europe faces the half-naked forms of Asia, Africa and America, a visual symbol of European superiority; above, the peace and justice of Christianity replaces the pagan past; frontispiece to book V of Braun and Hogenberg.

NOVA TOTIUS ORBIS MAPPA, EX OPTIMIS AUCTORIBUS DESUMTA, Studio Petri Kerl.

41 The majestic van den Keere world map of 1611, in which the map has become a paper theatre of lands and oceans, peoples and cities, monarchs and explorers: the archetypal image of the Renaissance world.

world be silent: there is none to be paralleled to it', writes the geographer Janssen in his final edition of the Mercator-Hondius Atlas of 1636:

> Ye shall behold in her magnificent and high-steepled churches and temples, and an infinite number of abbeys, monasteries and hospitals, many excellent palaces of princes, innumerable fair and excellent houses of great lords. … Here we have the right of laws, the dignity of the Christian religion, the force of arms, and infinite number of grave senators and counsellors. … Moreover Europe manageth all arts and sciences with such dexterity that for the invention of many things she may truly be called a mother, and for the conservation of many rare things, to bear the title a nursing mother of human wisdom: she hath in her most excellent academies for all manner of learning, whereas other countries are all of them overspread with barbarism. In fine, one cannot relate fully the virtues and qualities spoken of before.[2]

This was how the scholars and rulers of Renaissance Europe saw their culture, and how they saw themselves as the leaders of it. They were the civilized elite of the world, armed with virtue, courage, intelligence and judgement. It was a mere tautology to speak of European civilization: Europe *was* civilization, there was no other elsewhere in the world. This was a sophisticated culture, which liked to explore and reflect on its own qualities and codes of thought and conduct, and it was a culture which found its reflection in great works of literature and drama. Love, honesty, nobility, wit, pride, grace, self-doubt, treachery, cowardice, deceit, penitence, magnanimity – all these and more merged, separated and merged again to form an almost limitless range of human behaviour and emotion. This was the living drama that was presented by Shakespeare in personal relationships of attraction and conflict, played out within the context of European social life, in court, city and countryside. Sensational action or adventure rarely interested him for its own sake. Action there certainly was – warfare, plots, battles, truces, victories, defeats, reconciliations – but these actions were of interest because they took place in the minds and the hearts of men and women who were noble in reason, infinite in faculty, admirable, angelic, god-like, the beauty of the world – at least potentially. This catalogue of virtues was Shakespeare's ironic comment on the European Renaissance ideal of man, an ideal which he probes, dissects, frequently tears apart, but also, in some part at least, restores.

The world beyond Europe contributes an interesting range of images into the plays. The subhuman creatures whom Othello saw, 'whose heads / Do grow beneath their shoulders',[3] appear on the maps of Africa and Asia, as does the homeland of the 'barbarous Scythian' condemned with such horror by Lear, while cannibals, Othello's 'anthropophagi', seem to roam on ancient maps throughout the savage world, from Siberia to South America. Prester John, the legendary Christian king, whose kingdom shifted between India and Africa, is mentioned by Benedick in *Much Ado* along with the 'great Cham', in other words the Great Khan of China. All these were survivals from medieval beliefs, and had been shown on the great *mappae mundi* like the one preserved in Hereford. Closer to home in the Elizabethan age, Falstaff's tenacious pursuit of Mistress Ford and Mistress Page in *The Merry Wives of Windsor* is purely mercenary, and he proclaims

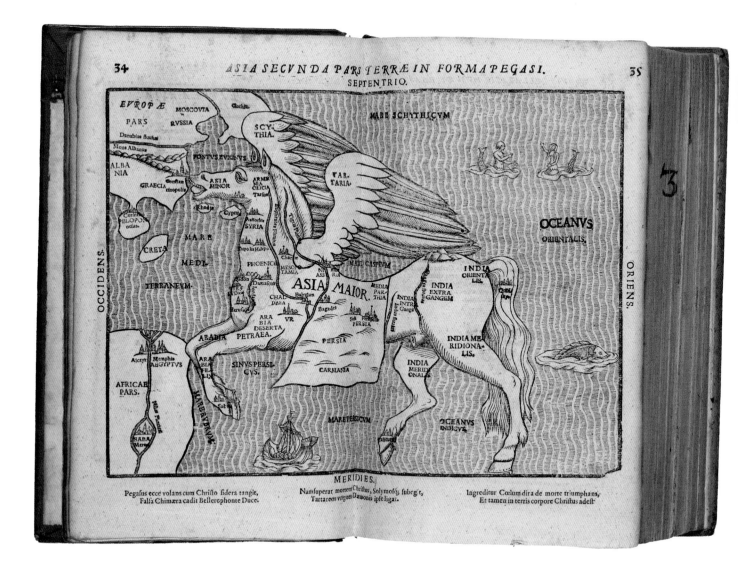

34

SEPTENTRIO.

EVROPÆ PARS
MOSCOVIA RVSSIA
Gachis
Danubius fluuius
Mons Albanus
ALBANIA
GRAECIA
Constantinopolis
PONTVS EVXINVS
ASIA MINOR
ARMENIA CILICIA
Tarfus
Rhodus
Cyprus
SCYTHIA.
MARE SCYTHICVM
TARTARIA.
OCEANVS ORIENTALIS.
Corinthus PELOPONesus
CRETA
Antiochia
SYRIA
Tripoli Halepo
Charan
PHOENICE
MESOPOTAMIA
MARE CASPIVM
INDIA ORIENTALIS.
MARE MEDITERRANEVM
Sidon
Damascus
Iudæa
Ierufalem
ASSYRIA
ASIA MAIOR
MEDIA PARTHIA
INDIA EXTRA GANGEM
INDIA INTRA Gangem
Babylon
CHALDAEA
Bagadet
Sol Perfepolis PERSIA
ARABIA DESERTA PETRAEA.
VR
Alcayr
Memphis AEGYPTVS
ARABIA FELIX.
SINVS PERSICVS.
PERSIA
INDIA MERIDIONALIS.
CARMANIA
AFRICAE PARS.
Nilus Fluuius
MARE RVBRVM
INDIA MERIDIONALIS.
OCEANVS INDICVS.
SABA Meroe
MARE PERSICVM

MERIDIES.

Pegasus ecce volans cum Christo sidera tangit, Falsa Chimæra cadit Bellerophonte Duce.

Nam superat mortem Christus, Solymosq; subeg't, Tartareos vngues Dæmonis ipse ligat.

Ingreditur Cœlum dira de morte triumphans, Et tamen in terris corpore Christus adest.

35

42 A curious symbolic map published by Heinrich Bünting in 1598. Pegasus' flight into the heavens becomes a symbol of Christ's resurrection and ascension; Asia was the site of God's self-revelation to mankind, but is now in the hands of Muslims; this image can therefore be read as an attempt to reclaim Asia for Christianity.

proudly that to him they will be 'a region in Guiana, all gold and bounty … they shall be my East and West Indies, and I will trade to them both.'[4] This is a direct reference to Sir Walter Raleigh's book *The Discovery of the Large, Rich and Beautiful Empire of Guiana* of 1595, based on his exploration of the Orinoco in search of the fabled El Dorado.

Shakespeare was writing exactly a hundred years after the first discovery of the New World that lay on the other side of the Atlantic, and after the Portuguese had rounded the southern tip of Africa and opened the eastern sea route to India. It was the greatest revolution in geographical knowledge in the history of the world, yet its intellectual impact was small. It was seen as essentially military and commercial, a chance for the two great seafaring powers, Spain and Portugal, to seize on vast new sources of materials and wealth in gold, silver and spices. In terms of re-evaluating human culture it was insignificant, for the races encountered in the New World were regarded as naked savages, fit only to be exploited and enslaved; to many it was even a question whether they possessed souls, and whether they could therefore be seen as human. The New Worlds reached by the eastern and western sea routes were quickly divided by papal decree between the two Iberian nations, and the other European nations could only look on with envy. This situation changed after the Reformation, when defiance of Spain and Portugal became a desirable political goal, and first Britain then the Netherlands attacked their overseas empires. Anti-Spanish feeling in Protestant England was a powerful force, and Drake was the great English hero who, virtually single-handed, propelled England into the quest for overseas trade and colonies, in the course of which Spanish power was to be at least cut down, if not destroyed.

The great world maps of the late sixteenth century built a new image of the world, firstly in the sense that the hugely enlarged land area of the globe was newly mapped in detail, but secondly in the sense that the map is encrusted with images of European power. Ships, navigators and monarchs crowd the oceans; symbolic figures of the continents of Africa, Asia and America are invariably shown paying homage to that of Europe; tableaux showing the four classical elements, the four seasons, the seven wonders of the world, and views of the world's cities extend around the edges. The world map became a paper theatre in which European monarchs, princes, explorers and merchants could contemplate their spheres of power. Detached intellectual interest in the newly discovered lands and peoples of the world was virtually non-existent. It was the secular power of Renaissance man, supported by his superior techniques of navigation and warfare, that was being celebrated on these maps. There has been a great deal of discussion – connected primarily with *The Tempest* – which seeks to link Shakespeare with the New World and with European colonialism. Yet, while it is evident that Shakespeare was very well aware of this worldwide revolution in travel, exploration and discovery, he did not build any intellectual or dramatic structures upon it. His interest lay always in psychology, passion, intellect, wit and poetry – the things of the spirit – and none of this would work outside Europe.

The drama of the sea itself, however, did interest Shakespeare, its capacity for changing lives, for bringing misery or transformation, death or rebirth, and this motif informs a number of plays, especially the late romances. Shakespeare's theatre was justly called The Globe, for in his hands the drama represented the world in microcosm, but it was always the world of civilization, the European world.

But the great European ideal had one great flaw, namely the national and dynastic rivalries that kept the continent in a state of almost permanent warfare; indeed warfare nobly conducted with courage and honour was part of that civilization. But warfare always requires the denigration of one's enemies, and even learned geographers like Hondius and Janssen would eagerly rehearse popular prejudices:

> The Francons are simple, blockish and furious; the Bavarians
> sumptuous gluttons and brazen-faced; the Swedes light,
> babblers and boasters; the Thuringians distrustful, slovens
> and quarrelsome; the Saxons dissemblers, double-hearted and
> opinionative; the Belgians good horsemen, tender, docible
> and delicate; the Italians proud, revengeful and ingenious;
> the Spaniard disdainful, cautious and greedy; the Gauls
> proper, intemperate, rash-headed, the Cimbrians high-minded,
> seditious and terrible; the Sarmates gluttons, proud and
> thieves; the Bohemians cruel, lovers of novelties, filtchers; the
> Illyrics variable, malicious and riotous; the Pannonians rude,
> superstitious; the Grecians miserable. Briefly, there is another
> gentle form to express these vices by: a pont of Polonia, a monk
> of Bohemia, a warrior of Austria, a religious Swede, Italian
> devotion, Prussian religion, a German breakfast, the French
> constancy – all of them not worth a nut.[5]

This is an essential stratum of popular lore – that foreigners are different, and in their lands things happen that could never here at home; this was clearly a doctrine that could be highly useful to a dramatist. Places exist in the imagination as well as in reality, even more perhaps in the imagination, and a play set in Italy, Bohemia, France or Denmark clearly carried a certain weight of expectation, even before the first curtain had risen.

Italy: the setting

IN THE EUROPE of the sixteenth century, by common consent the crown of the civilized ideal was Italy. Italy had inherited the prestige of Rome, she was the centre of Christendom, she had been reborn in the Renaissance, and in Shakespeare's time her cities led the world for physical magnificence and sophistication of social life. As Europe was to the world, so Italy was to Europe, as the geographers proclaimed:

> A country hallowed by the gods, the happiest and best of all
> Europe, a princess over all nations, a queen of the world, yea
> the nurse and parent of all regions, elected by the providence
> of the gods to make the heavens more famous, to gather
> the scattered empires of the world into one body, to temper
> the barbarous rites of nations, to unite so many disagreeing
> languages of men by the benefit of one common tongue, and in
> a word to restore man to humanity.[6]

Significantly this passage quoted by Janssen in his *Atlas* is from Pliny: the Renaissance geographer saw no reason to diminish these words of praise written more than a thousand years earlier. He adds a more up-to-date note by citing the popular epithets that were attached to the chief Italian cities: 'Venice the rich, Milan the great, Genoa the proud, Florence the fair, Bologna the fertile, Ravenna the old, Rome the holy, and Naples the noble.' There are half a dozen plays which are located in these or in other slightly smaller cities like Padua and Verona, and one, *Twelfth Night*, in which Italy is exported across the Adriatic to Illyria. In these plays a royal

43 Shakespeare's Italy from the Münster Ptolemy atlas of 1540: from Syracuse and Messina to Rome, Venice, Verona, Padua and Milan, and Ragusa beyond the Adriatic, all Shakespeare's dramas are located here.

court is the setting for part of the action, or is in the background as a focus of social power, as in *Romeo and Juliet*. *The Taming of the Shrew* is the exception, being a bourgeois comedy throughout, as *The Merry Wives of Windsor* is in an English setting. In *Much Ado*, the court, in the person of the Prince Don Pedro, comes to a private house. Only *Hamlet* takes place from beginning to end in a royal household.

The contemporary state of Italy was of course highly problematic. It was not a nation-state as Britain, France or Spain was, but was divided into half a dozen leading regional powers and many more principalities and city-states, which were often at war with each other or prey to foreign powers. Since the Reformation had shattered the spiritual unity of Europe, Protestant writers could not in conscience argue for the continuity of the Catholic lands with true Christianity, which they claimed to be the distinguishing mark of European civilization. Yet somehow the prestige of Italy survived these complicated problems, so that her culture was recognized as being on a superior plane:

> The Italians are lovers of learning, arts and sciences, for
> the advancement whereof they have made many excellent
> universities at Rome, Milan, Bologna, Padua, Pavia, Naples,
> Perugia, Salerno, Pisa, Ferrara, Sienna, Florence, Venice,
> Bergamo, Modena and Turin. To number up all the learned
> men that have flourished in Italy were impossible for me. In
> their manners, behaviours and gestures, the Italians are very
> civil, courteous and gentle, surpassing all other nations in merry
> conceits and pleasant discourses. They are of good capacity,
> apprehension and understanding, apt to learn and invent
> anything, ready-handed and teachable in all studies, arts and
> sciences. But from all antiquity they have been always ambitious
> and vainglorious, yea from the very breasts they have sucked in
> lusts as milk, being much inclined to idleness, a delicious life
> and venery.[7]

As for the women of Italy, they are 'magpies at the door, saints in the church, goddesses in the garden, devils in the house, angels in the streets, and sirens in the windows'. With the love sonnets of Petrarch and the novels of Boccaccio, Italy had revolutionized secular literature as her artists had revolutionized painting, sculpture and architecture.

It was Italy which produced the two outstanding practical guides to the Renaissance ideals of life, in Machiavelli's *The Prince* and Castiglione's *The Courtier*, written within a few years of each other, and immensely influential throughout Europe. *The Prince* was the first treatise of realpolitik, an unashamed defence of the principle that the sole business of any ruler is

44 Engraving of *The Court of Love* by Francesco del Cossa, *c.*1470, which seems the perfect visual expression of the world of *Romeo and Juliet, Much Ado* and *Twelfth Night*.

power, and not the pursuit of any pretended social or moral enlightenment. In the pursuit and retention of power, any tactics are justified which give strength and stability to the prince, and there is no higher tribunal to which his enemies, or history, can appeal to condemn him. The Machiavellian character is ruthless and self-regarding, exploiting the scruples and the weaknesses of others. Consequently he was easily seen as an iconic figure of evil, a devilish force standing in opposition to any standards of honesty, morality or religion.

To be fair to Machiavelli, his detractors often overlooked the fact that he wrote the book with a specific purpose, namely to inspire an Italian ruler with the strength and determination to resist, to outmanoeuvre and to expel the foreign powers that meddled continually in Italian affairs. Only a determined and ruthless leader could hope to achieve this. Power was not pursued merely to satisfy personal instincts of aggression, but as an instrument of state politics in which the end justifies the means. The prince must be able to imitate the lion or the fox, and he should have no other objectives or concerns except war, its methods and practices. Thus Machiavelli throws down the challenge of realpolitik to the classical and humanist traditions that a prince should display qualities such as generosity, magnanimity and clemency. That Shakespeare must have known the character and message of this famous book is certain, even if he had never read it himself (there was a partial English translation in 1602 but no full one until 1640), since he has the future Richard III say that he will 'set the murd'rous Machiavel to school'.[8]

The other fundamental guide to Italian Renaissance social ideas was the utterly different *Courtier* by Castiglione, first published in 1528. This classic text takes the form of a series of colloquies at the court of Urbino, in which a group of nobles, all named historical figures, are hosted by Elisabetta Gonzago in a free discussion of the ideal qualities that make up a courtier, male or female. These are beauty of appearance, physical dexterity, courage, learning and wit, and above all the elusive quality of grace, of being able to carry all these things off with effortless ease, and without affection or boastfulness. One whole section of the book is devoted to language, the manner of addressing oneself to one's friends or to one's prince with elegance and liveliness, with jests and wordplay. *The Courtier* must be seen as part of a civilizing process away from the cruel tyrannies of the medieval courts and towards the more elegant, fastidious social code of the Renaissance. The book was one of the great bestsellers of its age: in the first ninety years after its publication it was issued in no less than 110 editions, sixty in Italy and fifty overseas, including translations into French, German, Spanish and Polish. The English version by Sir Thomas Hoby appeared in 1561.

The language of courtly greetings and expressions of respect that we find throughout Shakespeare's plays is partly indebted to Castiglione – it was as much a mark of good breeding as one's clothing – while the glittering repartee that darts back and forth is recommended by Castiglione as an art that can be learned, although some in the discussion group disagree, affirming that it is a gift. It works by a form of punning, by seizing on a word and developing the ideas it suggests in a new and surprising sense, so that keeping the conversation going becomes competitive, like keeping a shuttlecock in the air. Castiglione gives many amusing examples, but none as swift and deadly as those which Shakespeare puts into the mouths of Beatrice and Benedick or Rosaline and Berowne. Of course those on the receiving end smart under the attack, as when Benedick exclaims to Beatrice, 'I would my horse had the speed of your tongue'.[9] This form of dialogue reveals character without advancing the action. By contrast there can be a more functional kind of dialogue which, although rapid and subtle, does not exist solely to draw attention to itself, but clearly moves the play forward, for example King Edward's wooing of Lady Grey in part III of *Henry VI*. The wit of courtly wordplay was an art, and as such was one of the refinements of civilized life. Castiglione recommended that in times of peace, warlike attitudes must be set aside in order to cultivate these refinements. Significantly, Machiavelli's view was grimmer and more prosaic: 'It is evident that when rulers concern themselves more with the refinements of life than with military matters, they lose power.'[10]

The figure of the Machiavellian villain was placed on the Elizabethan stage and given truly outrageous comic form by Marlowe in *The Jew of Malta*. Machiavelli himself is made to speak the Prologue, with its notorious lines: 'I count religion but a childish toy / And hold there is no sin but ignorance.'[11] Even popes, he boasts, have risen to the chair of St Peter by studying his works, and any rulers who ignore him are in danger of being eliminated by their more ambitious followers. He claims his soul has flown beyond the Alps to England, and entered the body of the play's main character, Barabas the Jew, whose profession and delight is murder, preferably of Christians. This, however, is the kind of caricature which gave Machiavelli such a bad name, since Barabas's motives are personal and pathological, and not concerned with political power at all. He brings the Machiavellian villain nearer to home in *The Massacre at Paris* (a play known imperfectly through a mangled text) in the character of the Duke of Guise, instigator of the St Bartholomew's Day massacre of 1572. Strangely perhaps, Marlowe does not set a play in Italy. Shakespeare gives us more believable Machiavellian villains in Richard III and Edmund in *King Lear*, while Iago in *Othello* and Angelo in *Measure for Measure* could both be seen as Machiavellians of the personal passions. It is noticeable that there are no Machiavels in the Roman plays, this character being at odds with Roman ideals. One play in which Shakespeare evidently had both Castiglione and Machiavelli in mind is *Much Ado About Nothing*, in the figures respectively of the graceful Don Pedro and his malevolent brother, Don John.

The English perception of and response to Italy was a mixture of bafflement, wonder and deep moral disapproval, although this may have masked a certain envy at the liberties which Italians allowed themselves. The bafflement arose from the difficulty of understanding what Italy was, without a king, a capital, a unified language or a currency, and

45 The encounter between the English traveller Thomas Coryate and a Venetian courtesan; without such an encounter, no trip to Italy was complete, but Coryate claimed he had no purpose but to reform the woman. From Coryate's *Crudities*, 1611.

divided among innumerable political units that were fierce in their claims to independence and ardent in their local patriotism. When returning travellers reported this situation, they portrayed the many cities as states and as cultural islands with highly distinct identities, as indeed they were. For Shakespeare and other dramatists, this was a significant conception, to which they responded by treating places like Verona, Milan, Padua or Messina as if they were self-sufficient, enclosed worlds, with their own laws, customs and leading figures. The sentence of banishment from a city, for example, seemed almost tantamount to death to both Romeo and Valentine. One English commentator, Fynes Moryson, mocked the Italians for their parochialism, 'the great part of them having never seen the villages and towns within five or ten miles of their native soil'.[12] Each of these separate worlds began and ended at the city gates, rather as the play began and ended at the gates of the theatre. Unlike the English plays, there is no sense of Italian nationhood at work anywhere. The English, with their idea of the nation united in its belief in and loyalty to the Crown, felt that Italy was, in some sense at least, chaotic. This sense of bafflement still afflicts anyone today attempting to grasp the history of Italy during the Middle Ages and the Renaissance. It was reflected in the content of travel books like that of Fynes Moryson, who made extensive journeys in the 1590s and published his *Itinerary* some years afterwards. Moryson deals with the laws and customs of each city and region in turn as if he were describing a new country, and his lengthy text can certainly be seen as giving us a picture of parts of Shakespeare's Europe.

The wonder at things Italian was both positive and negative. In the first place, as Moryson admits, Italy's supremacy in all things artistic was undisputed: 'For painting, sculpture, or carving in brass and stone, and for architecture, they have been of old and still are most skilful masters, and whatsoever or any nations on this side of the Alps can do in these arts, they have learned it from them.'[13] Michelangelo's achievements were legendary, and were singled out by Moryson and every other travel writer, but Italian artistic excellence went down the scale to the making of jewels, silks, furniture and musical instruments. Their music itself, its composition and performance, Moryson praises in lyrical terms: 'In consorts of grave solemn music, sometimes running so sweetly with soft touching of the strings as may seem to ravish the hearer's spirit from his body.'[14] This takes us directly to Orsino's passion in *Twelfth Night*, to the sweet sounds conjured by Ariel on Prospero's island, and perhaps even to the idea of the healing power of music found in *Pericles* and *King Lear*. Another art in which the Italians excelled was verbal grace and wit, and here Moryson seems to echo the principles of Castiglione: 'By sweetness of language and singular art in seasoning their talk and behaviour with great ostentation of courtesy, they make their conversation sweet and pleasing to all men, easily gaining the goodwill of those with whom they live.'[15] It was these outstanding artistic gifts and social graces which made Italian fashions so influential throughout Europe.

46 An Italian conversation piece that brings instantly to mind the picture of Othello disputing with Iago, Cassio, Roderigo and Montano. Frontispiece to Braun and Hogenberg, book V.

But this grace and style came at a price, and Moryson devotes ample space to the vices and shortcomings of the Italians. Firstly, they have little prowess as soldiers or sailors, the latter fault especially calling up Moryson's scorn:

> The Italians, the old conquerors of the world, are at this day so effeminate and so enamoured of their paradise of Italy, as nothing but desperate fortune can make them undertake any voyages by sea or land … or any warfare by sea or land, or any hard course of life. And as generally they are reputed not very confident in God's protection by land, so they less trust him at sea, thinking that man to have had a heart of oak and brass who first dared to make furrows upon the waves of the sea, having nothing but a board between him and ugly death. So they seldom prove expert and never bold mariners.[16]

47 Four Italian characters from Cesare Vecellio's *Degli Habiti Antichi et Moderni*, 1590: A maiden in love – Juliet? A fashionable youth – Romeo? A Venetian senator – Brabantio? A superior Moor – Othello?

The reverse side of this attributed cowardice was the Italians readiness for violence, factional fighting, honour killing and the like. Moryson illustrates this with a specific story concerning the Duke of Mantua when he was a youth:

> This prince one night walked the streets with his followers but unknown, and by ill adventure meeting a Scottish gentleman well reputed in his father's court, took a fancy to try his valour, and to that end commanded one of his familiar friends to assault him with his drawn sword; whom he, taking for an enemy in good earnest, resisted valiantly, and at the first encounter happened to give him a deadly wound; whereupon the prince much lamented, and the Scottish gentleman knowing him by his voice and so humbling himself at his feet, with tender of his rapier the point towards himself, the prince in rage killed him with his own weapon.[17]

This instantly brings to mind the unpremeditated fight in *Romeo and Juliet* that leaves two people dead in the street, and it prepares us for much more that Moryson has to say about the dangers of the ungoverned Italian character. For such offences, men fled or were banished from the cities to become *banditi*, living on woodlands outside the confines, 'committing robberies and murders with strange examples of cruelty', unless they can find a way to bribe or buy their way to forgiveness by the authorities, sometimes by killing rival *banditi*. These are the rather gentlemanly outlaws shown in *The Two Gentlemen of Verona*, haunting the woods between Milan and Verona, until the all-powerful Duke pardons them. In fear of both street attacks and of *banditi*, Moryson reports that to his personal knowledge many young gentlemen go armed from head to foot, and that 'they wear continually an iron coat of mail of thirty pounds weight next to their shirts'. The time of the carnivals, he says, is a particularly nervous one for those who walk the streets by night, rapiers and lanterns being the essential order of the day.

The other great motive for violence was of course the passion of love:

> Adulteries (as all furies of jealousy or signs of making love
> to wives, daughters and sisters) are commonly prosecuted by
> private revenge and by murder, and the princes and judges,
> measuring their just revenge by their own passion proper to that
> nation, make no great enquiry after such murders, besides that
> the revenging party is wise enough to do them secretly, or at
> least in disguised habits.[18]

This recalls Othello's instant decision that Desdemona's adultery deserves death, although clearly he had not the coolness to disguise his actions. Revenge, says Moryson, is seen as merely justice operating in secret. In Italian literature the best-known case of murder for adultery is probably that of Paolo Malatesta and Francesca da Rimini, killed by the vengeful husband, Gianciotto, and immortalized by Dante in canto 5 of the *Inferno*. The dagger was favoured, but an alternative way was always poison:

> For poisons the Italians' skill in making and putting them to
> use hath been long since tried, to the perishing of kings and
> emperors by those deadly potions given to them in the very

chalice mingled with the precious blood of our redeemer …
In our time it seems the art of poisoning is reputed in
Italy worthy of princes' practice. For I could name a prince
among them who having composed an exquisite poison and
counterpoison, made proof of them both upon condemned
men, giving the poison to all and the counterpoison only to
some condemned for less crimes, till he had found out the work
of both to a minute of time, upon divers complexions and ages
of men.[19]

This is the world of *Romeo and Juliet*, *Hamlet* and *King Lear*, as well as
Marlowe's *The Jew of Malta*. In his *Edward II*, Marlowe's exquisite murderer
Lightborn boast of his Italian training in the art of killing in secret:

I learned in Naples how to poison flowers;
To strangle with a lawn thrust through the throat;
To pierce the windpipe with a needle's point;
Or whilst one is asleep, to take a quill
And blow a little powder in his ears,
Or open his mouth and pour quicksilver down.[20]

The passions of love, jealousy and revenge lead Moryson on to a shocked
description of the more basic instincts that lie behind them:

For fleshly lusts, the very Turks (whose carnal religion alloweth
them) are not so much transported therewith as the Italians
are, in their restraint of civil laws and the dreadful law of God.
A man of these northerly parts can hardly believe without the
testimony of his own eyes and ears how chastity is laughed
at among them, and hissed out of all good company, or how
desperate adventures they will make to achieve disordinate
desires in these kinds.[21]

This is true not only with the men, who are 'carried with fierce affections
to forbidden lusts', but the women too, even wives and virgins being in
Italy 'much sooner inflamed with love, be it lawful or unlawful, than the
women of other nations'. Is this King Lear speaking, or Hamlet, or Othello,
or Leontes? This picture is crowned by Moryson's survey of prostitution
as a profession:

Fornication in Italy is not a sin winked at, but rather may be called an allowed trade, for princes and states raise great tribute from it. At Naples each poor courtesan pays to the prince two carlines to the month, besides greater extortions upon those that are fair, and having great and many lovers, grow proud in apparel and rich in purse, and the number of harlots was thought to exceed sixty thousand. At Venice the tribute to the state from courtesans was thought to exceed 300,000 crowns yearly, and the Pope's holiness made no less gain from this fair trade at Rome.[22]

We may well gasp at Moryson's statistics, which would seem to make three-quarters of the female population of Naples harlots. But, allowing for exaggeration, these passages take us to the sordid brothel scenes in *Measure for Measure* and *Pericles*, and again to Marlowe's Malta and the outrageous Bellamira.

So the balance sheet on Italy which we can draw up from Moryson's memoirs is this: Italy is stylish, artistic, hedonistic, colourful, exciting and dangerous. As the setting for dramatic action, this could scarcely be more enticing: it is sophisticated and European, but utterly un-English, a place where confusion and passion can have full sway, where anything can happen.

Italy: the plays

THE ARCHETYPAL Italian court comedy of love and intrigue, deception, conflict and joyful resolution is *Much Ado About Nothing*. The setting is Messina in Sicily, a location which Shakespeare found in his source, a novella by Matteo Bandello that was published in 1554. This contains the Claudio–Hero story only, for the Beatrice–Benedick element was apparently invented by Shakespeare himself. But alongside the dazzling language of the verbal ballet between these two – the Castiglione element – we are shown the scheming of the pathological Don John, the cold, hateful brother of the governor Don Pedro. Don John has rebelled against Don Pedro, been defeated and apparently reconciled with him. Yet he is still a bitter malcontent, and ruthlessly sets out to wreck the wedding between Hero and Claudio, the latter his brother's lieutenant and friend. Very different from Marlowe's Barabas, Don John is nevertheless clearly a Machiavellian figure, brooding, calculating and entirely amoral in pursuit of his ends. Sicily is indeed the perfect setting for this element of the drama, for the island's political history for three centuries before Shakespeare lived was a confused and violent succession of dynastic wars and internecine quarrels within the ranks of its foreign rulers – Norman, German, Angevin and Aragonese. The conflict between Don Pedro and Don John has no exact historical counterpart, but is entirely credible, and the name Pedro commemorates Pedro of Aragon, the first Spanish ruler of Sicily after the French had been expelled following the notorious massacre known as the Sicilian Vespers in 1282; it was Pedro who entered Messina in

48 (*overleaf*) Messina and the Straits, from Braun and Hogenberg, 1617, with the smoke of Mount Etna far too close to the city – it is more than 50 kilometres away.

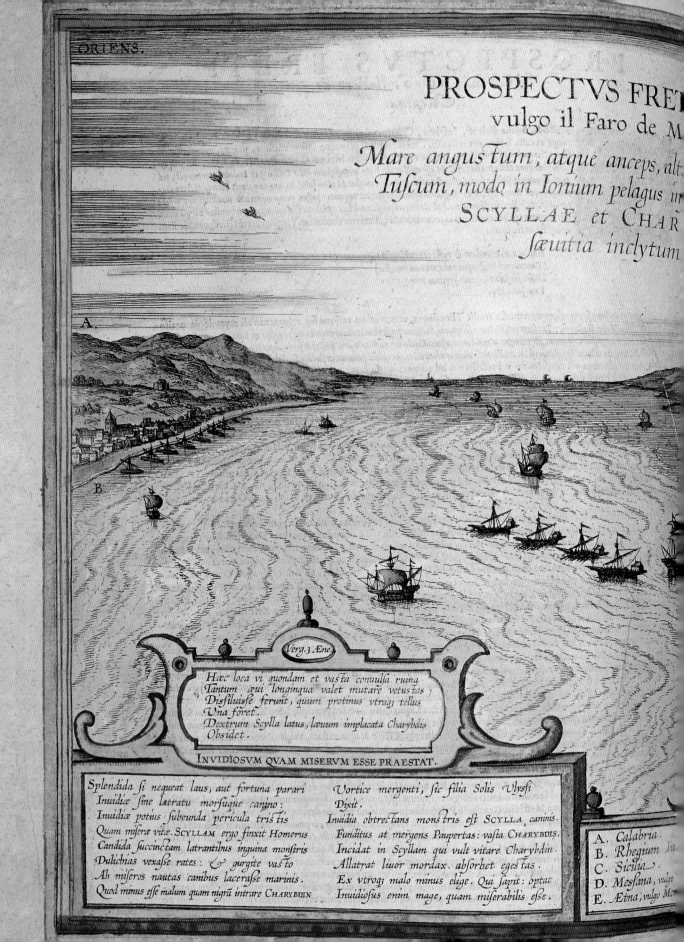

PROSPECTVS FRE
vulgo il Faro de M

Mare angustum, atque anceps, alt
Tuscum, modo in Ionium pelagus in
SCYLLAE et CHAR
saeuitia inclytum

A.

B.

Verg. 3 Aene.

Haec loca vi quondam et vasta conuulsa ruina
(Tantum aeui longinqua valet mutare vetustas)
Dissiluisse ferunt, quum protinus vtraq; tellus
Vna foret.
Dextrum Scylla latus, laeuum implacata Charybdis
Obsidet.

INVIDIOSVM QVAM MISERVM ESSE PRAESTAT.

Splendida si nequeat laus, aut fortuna parari	*Vortice mergenti, sic filia Solis Vlyssi*
Inuidiae sine latratu morsuque canino:	*Dixit.*
Inuidiae potius subeunda pericula tristis	*Inuidia obtrectans monstris est* SCYLLA *caninis.*
Quam miserae vitae. SCYLLAM *ergo finxit Homerus*	*Funditus at mergens Paupertas: vasta* CHARYBDIS.
Candida succinctam latrantibus inguina monstris	*Incidat in Scyllam qui vult vitare Charybdin.*
Dulichias vexasse rates: & gurgite vasto	*Allatrat liuor mordax, absorbet egestas.*
Ah miseros nautas canibus lacerasse marinis.	*Ex vtroq; malo minus elige. Qui sapit: optat*
Quod minus esse malum quam nigrâ intrare CHARYBDIN	*Inuidiosus enim mage, quam miserabilis esse.*

A. *Calabria.*
B. *Rhegium*
C. *Sicilia*
D. *Messana, vulgo*
E. *Aetna, vulgo Mo*

CVLI,

...su modo in
...rticosum:

E.

C.

D.

...rcum inter studia aytographa
...ri Bruegelij Pictoris nostri
...li eximij. Ab ipsomet deline-
...m. Communicauit Georgius
...ufnaglius Anno 1617.

triumph after his victory over the French. More tenuous historically, it may not be entirely irrelevant to recall that the Straits of Messina were reputedly the location of Scylla and Charybdis, the legendary monster and the nearby whirlpool celebrated and feared by sailors; the perception of Sicily as a place of danger, treachery and antagonism had a long history.

That same aura hangs over the court of King Leontes in the other Sicilian play, *The Winter's Tale*. Critics have noticed that the language of

49 Sicily from Münster's *Cosmographia*, 1552.

the Sicilian scenes contains many images of winter, desolation and death, in contrast to the Bohemian scenes, the realm of King Polixenes, which are full of vernal and pastoral images of life and joy. The source text was the novel *Pandosto, or the Triumph of Time*, by Robert Greene, published in 1588. Geographically the interesting point is that Shakespeare reversed the original locations; in the novel the jealous Leontes character, Pandosto, is King of Bohemia, and Egistus, corresponding to Polixenes, is King

50 Encircled by its hills and forests, Bohemia is shown as the heart – or stomach – of Europe, by Heinrich Bünting, 1598.

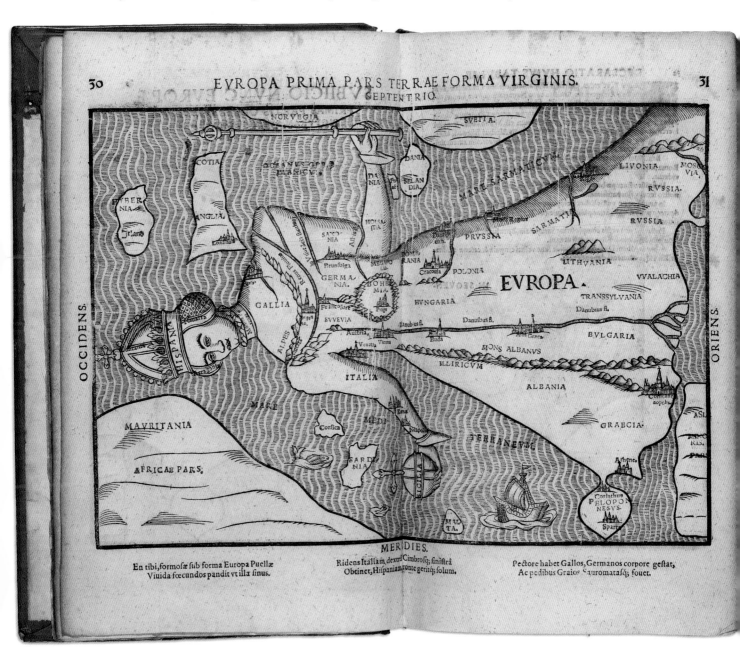

EVROPA PRIMA PARS TERRAE FORMA VIRGINIS.

51 Pygmalion from a German edition of Ovid, 1569; the story of a statue brought to life to become the lover of its creator may have inspired the final scene of *The Winter's Tale*.

of Sicilia. However, having made this alteration, did Shakespeare forget his geography, since he created the famous puzzle of having Perdita and Antigonus being cast out upon the coast of Bohemia, where he should have written Sicilia? Unfortunately it is not as simple as that, for in *Pandosto* Bohemia too is described as a coastal state: Egistus and his men 'got to the sea shore, where with many a bitter curse, they took their leave of Bohemia'. So, although it is inconceivable that Shakespeare had no access to a map of Europe, he merely followed his source, and disregarded geography. Why the writers of Tudor or Stuart England should have imagined Bohemia as a coastal kingdom is impossible to explain.

The name Leontes must surely be taken from the town of Leontini, a Greek colony in the east of Sicily, mentioned by many classical authors. The lion was one of the emblems of Sicily, and the name appears again in Leonato ('Lion-born') of *Much Ado*. Another name in *The Winter's Tale* is more specific, more resonant and more puzzling: Giulio Romano, 'that rare Italian master',[23] is the only artist ever mentioned by Shakespeare, in whose works names like Michelangelo, Raphael, Titian or Tintoretto never appear. Giulio had been employed by the Gonzagas in Mantua, principally on the design and rich decoration of the Palazzo Te, and he was a polymath – painter, sculptor and architect. He had been a pupil of Raphael, and Shakespeare could certainly have seen his name in Vasari's celebrated book on the lives of the Italian artists, although no English translation of it then existed. But Giulio's subject matter was often erotic, and he was notorious for having drawn a series of plates for Aretino's *I Modi d'Amore*, arguably the first pornographic book ever published. In the context of the solemn and inspired 'resurrection' scene in the play, Giulio's name seems odd and out of place, but it must have been chosen as some kind of recherché allusion, whose significance would have been known to a select few.

It may seem strange that the sun-drenched Mediterranean island of Sicily should be associated with winter, with destruction and death, while the more northerly, landlocked region of Bohemia is shown as idyllic and pastoral, the setting of renewed life. Among the educated, Sicily was known and celebrated as the birthplace of Theocritus, the great master of pastoral poetry, and it was identified with his idylls. Yet Bohemia was also known as a rich pastoral land, a land of woods and rivers, to some extent cut off from its neighbours by the ring of forests and hills, virtually mountains, which surround the country. Contemporary maps show Bohemia in a faintly Edenic style, islanded by forests, while Heinrich Bunting's famous fantasy map of Europe transformed into the figure of a queen shows Bohemia as either the stomach or perhaps the slightly misplaced heart of the continent. If Shakespeare had a deliberate purpose in reversing the two locations, then perhaps it was because this feeling about Bohemia was in his mind. However, the point about Sicily in the play is that we don't see it directly: we see only Leontes's court, a place cut off from the idyllic countryside, a place of falsehood, suspicion and anger, a place where winter always reigns until the reconciliation scenes at the end, at which point Leontes says to Perdita and Florizel, 'Welcome hither, as the sun is to the earth.'[24] Perhaps too Shakespeare wished to move Leontes and his kingdom south, to bring it within the reaches of the Greek world, to make plausible the appeal to the oracle of Delphos. The Syracuse region of Sicily was originally a Greek colony, whereas Bohemia enters history as a medieval European

52 The name Illyria for the Dalmatian coast was still current on sixteenth-century maps; from the map of Greece by Nikolaos Sophianos, 1601.

kingdom, and in Shakespeare's time it was part of the Hapsburgs' Austrian dominions. The location of *The Winter's Tale* in time and in culture is certainly ambiguous, but it is clearly pagan rather than Christian, ancient or legendary rather than modern, and the idea of a Hapsburg Bohemian king offending the sacred Greek oracle is considerably less plausible than that of a Sicilian.

> *Viola*   What country, friends, is this?
> *Captain*   This is Illyria, lady.[25]

These lines from *Twelfth Night* constitute one of Shakespeare's most elegant and enticing pieces of scene setting, but one that is half-hidden in a

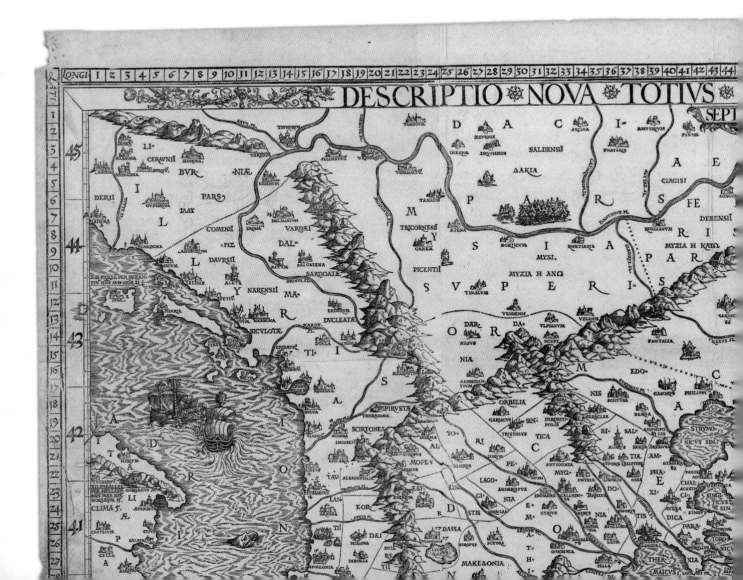

deliberate mist of uncertainty. Illyria was an ancient region of the northwestern Balkans, extending some hundreds of miles along the Adriatic coast from Istria down to modern-day Albania. It became a Roman province, and the emperors Diocletian and Constantine were both Illyrians; there Diocletian built his monumental palace at Split. From the thirteenth century until Shakespeare's time, this coast was under Venetian control, and by that time it was generally known as Dalmatia, although the name Illyria still appeared on maps of the sixteenth and seventeenth centuries. The character of *Twelfth Night* is entirely Italian, as are its literary sources – principally an anonymous play entitled *Gl'Ingannati* ('The Deceived') – but Shakespeare must have felt that he needed an unnamed setting, perhaps even a fantasy

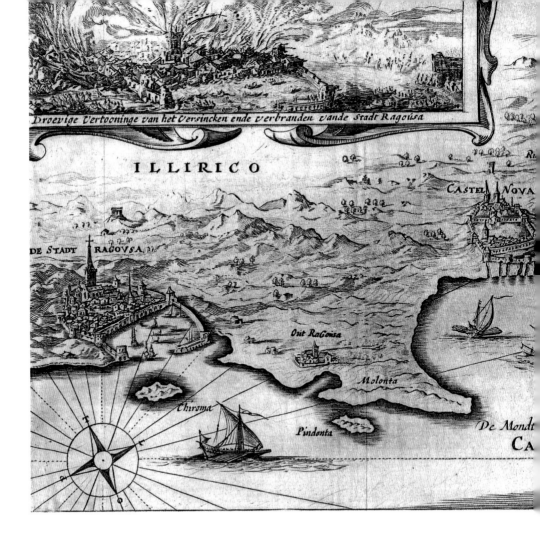

Droevige Vertooninge van het Versincken ende verbranden vande Stadt Ragousa

ILLIRICO

CASTEL NOVA

DE STADT RAGOVSA

Out RaGousa

Molonta

Chiroma

Pindonta

De Mondi
CA

53 Ragusa on the Dalmatian coast – today's Dubrovnik – an independent city-state and a possible model for Orsino's capital. This print refers to the earthquake which severely damaged the city in 1667.

world, for this wistful comedy of confused loves and confused identities. Perhaps the opening shipwreck, which he found in his sources, gave him the idea of shifting the scene beyond Italy, yet not far away, across the Adriatic. If Duke Orsino's capital had an original it is unknown, but there is one strong candidate in the city of Ragusa, the modern name of which is Dubrovnik. Ragusa was a major trading port and the only one to resist becoming subject to Venice, maintaining its independent status under the rule of its own Duke until the Napoleonic era. If Shakespeare intended Orsino's realm to be an independent city state on the Adriatic coast opposite Italy, Ragusa was the only model. The city was fabled for its maritime wealth, such that the word 'argosy' is derived from the Italian *Ragusea* – 'of Ragusa'. In 1667, the city was greatly damaged by an earthquake, a scene illustrated in many contemporary prints. All this is airy speculation, but it would not have been difficult for Shakespeare to have gleaned facts enough about Ragusa for it to blossom in his imagination into his Illyrian capital.

In the remaining Italian plays, the action is set variously in Padua, Verona or Milan. Padua was famous above all for its university, a medieval foundation of high repute, to which hundreds of Englishmen travelled over the years, especially to the medical school. William Harvey, who discovered the circulation of the blood, spent five years studying in Padua, and graduated from there in 1602. Benedick from *Much Ado* was said to be a native of Padua, while Petruchio from *The Taming of the Shrew* was not, being from Verona, and Katharina's nerve-wracking journeys to and from his house are presumed to be between the two cities. At the very opening of *The Shrew* Lucentio describes Padua as a 'nursery of arts', while Portia in *The Merchant of Venice* gets her lawyer's robes from her cousin Bellario in Padua. Could the name Bellario be an echo of that of the courtesan Bellamira in Marlowe's *The Jew of Malta*? It is Bellamira who says mockingly, 'From Padua / were

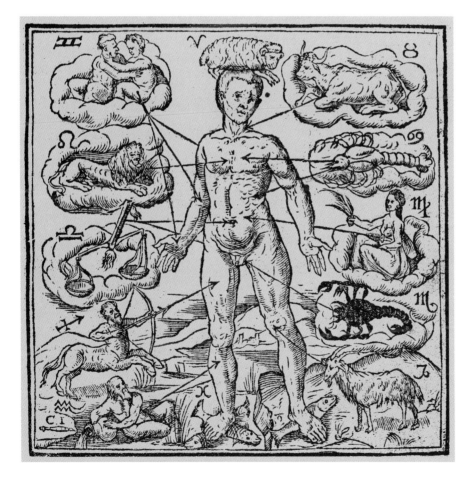

54 A 'Zodiac Man' diagram, illustrating the belief that each constellation governed one part of the body. It is mentioned in *Twelfth Night*, but Sir Toby and Sir Andrew are both wrong about the influence of Taurus; from a scientific treatise by Thomas Digges published in 1576.

55 Padua, from Braun and
Hogenberg, 1617.

wont to come rare-witted gentlemen, / scholars I mean, learned and liberal'.[26]
It seems that whenever English writers required a reference to scholarship or
a respected university, they reached for the name of Padua. The word had
become an aspect of fashion which audiences and readers would recognize,
a place to be seen in and to claim acquaintance with.

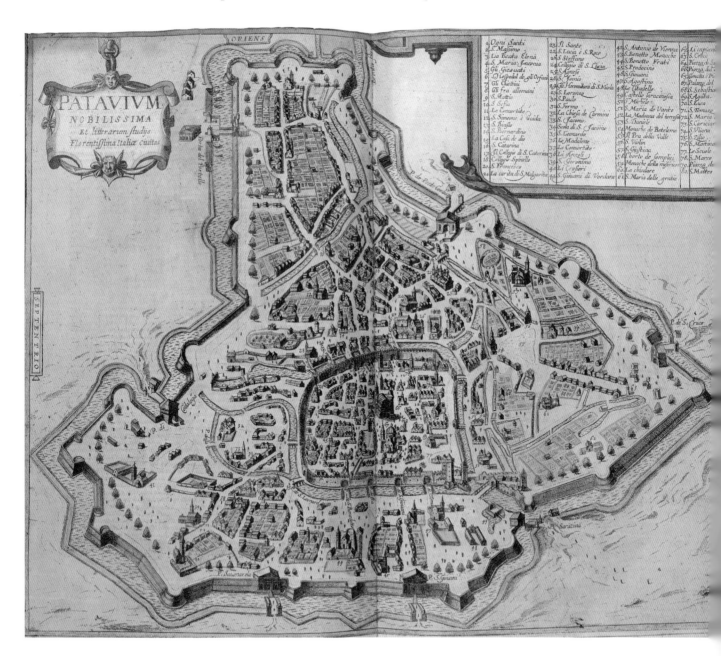

Two of the primary sources for *The Shrew* were the anonymous play *The Taming of the Shrew* and George Gascoigne's play *Supposes*. The setting of the first is Athens, and that of the second Ferrara. Therefore, as with Othello, we are justified in asking whether Shakespeare had a reason for transferring his version of the story to Padua. There is one obvious answer, namely that the entire Bianca–Lucentio story focuses on teaching as a pretext for wooing, while the Shrew's taming is also a training, a process of re-education. It seems perfectly fitting therefore that the university town of Padua should be chosen as the setting. Indeed it may be that Shakespeare is indulging in a subtle joke here at the expense of formal education, saying in effect that what happens to Bianca and Katharina forms an education in the university of life and love. Shakespeare made this same point explicitly in Berowne's great speech in *Love's Labour's Lost*, arguing that experience is a far greater teacher than academic study, and that the greatest experience of all is love.

Verona was well known to travellers as the first notable city to be reached on descending into Italy from the Brenner Pass. Its picturesque setting on the River Adige and its Roman arena were landmarks described in many travel texts, although the original tomb of Juliet, if it ever existed, was not. The tomb seen by modern tourists in the crypt off the Via Pallone is approximately of the right period, but it has no authentic history. The story of Romeo and Juliet was an ancient one. Dante himself in the *Purgatorio* lists the Montecchi and Cappelletti as being among those proud tyrants and patricians whose feuds hold the Italian cities in ceaseless unrest or mutual war. Many printed versions of the story, in Italian and French translations, were in circulation during the sixteenth century, and Shakespeare may have known some of them, but his principal source was the English poem *The Tragical History of Romeus and Juliet* by Arthur Brooke, published in 1562. Tedious to read, with its long wandering lines of alternating twelve and fourteen syllables, it provided a very full framework for the dramatist, with a great deal of detailed plotting and much local colour concerning the social life of Verona. The chief differences are that Brooke extends the action over many months, and that Shakespeare invents the celebrated characters of the Nurse and Mercutio. Brooke even opens with a prologue in the form of a sonnet, which evidently seemed an excellent idea to Shakespeare:

COLONIA AVGVS
TA VERONA NO
VA GALLIENIA
NA.

Love hath inflamèd twain by sudden sight.
And both do grant the thing that both desire.
They wed in shrift by counsel of a friar.
Young Romeus climbs fair Juliet's bower by night.
Three months he doth enjoy his chief delight.
By Tybalt's rage provokèd unto ire,
He payeth death to Tybalt for his hire.
A banished man, he 'scapes by secret flight.
New marriage is offered to his wife:
She drinks a drink that seems to reve her breath.
They bury her that, sleeping, yet hath life.
He drinks his bane. And she with Romeus knife,
When she awakes, herself alas she slaith.[27]

56 Verona, from Braun and
Hogenberg, 1581. The romantic
figures placed on the hillside
outside the city cannot fail to
remind us of Romeo and Juliet.

In the second Verona play, *The Two Gentlemen of Verona*, Shakespeare
rather strangely falls victim once again to his fondness for coasts, or at
least for a tidal and navigable river, since Valentine and Proteus travel

to Milan by ship, and Panthino exclaims to Launce, 'Away, ass! You'll lose the tide'.[28] After the first two acts of this play, we see no more of Verona, but instead the scene has shifted to the court of the Duke of Milan, or to the wild, bandit-infested wood said to lie between the two cities. Milan and Venice were the two leading powers in northern Italy, dominating the many smaller cities either through alliances or by outright force, and the Duke of Milan was one of the greatest figures in Italy. There is no real sense of Milan as a place in *The Two Gentlemen*, but its political history in the fourteenth and fifteenth centuries is of interest as suggesting the Milanese background to *The Tempest*. Dynastic conflict between and within the leading families was the central fact in the history of all the Italian states and cities, and Milan was no exception in the years when first the Visconti and then the Sforza were lords of the city and the duchy. Francesco Sforza took power by virtue of being the son-in-law of the last of the Visconti, but his children's succession proved disputed and bloody. The elder son, Galeazzo, was murdered in 1476, and his brother Ludovico, known as 'The Moor' for his swarthy appearance, was suspected by some as the instigator. Ludovico took over as regent to Galeazzo's young son, but soon afterwards the young heir mysteriously and conveniently died. His mother was exiled, and her advisors executed, leaving Ludovico master of the field, to preside over the Milanese Renaissance. These events – usurpation and murder – and others of a similar kind in many Italian cities seem to offer a model for the story of Prospero's fall and banishment from Milan. They could easily have been known to Shakespeare from histories of Italy such as that written by William Thomas and published in 1549, which became the authoritative work of its kind for the next half-century. As well as his great learning, Thomas was noted by his contemporaries for his 'hot, fiery spirit', and perhaps his many years residence in Italy developed in him a penchant for adventure and conspiracy, for he was executed for treason in 1554 for his part in the Wyatt conspiracy against Queen Mary Tudor.

57 (*overleaf*) Milan, from Braun and Hogenberg, 1572; the great ducal palace of the Sforzas, where acts 2 and 3 of *The Two Gentlemen of Verona* presumably take place, is in the north-centre.

The non-Italian plays

MEASURE FOR MEASURE has long been classified as one of Shakespeare's 'problem plays', in the double sense that it deals overtly with quite specific moral and psychological problems, but also that its structure and viewpoint are both problematic, ambivalent. The play's setting – it is the only one located in any of the Germanic countries – shares something of this enigmatic quality. The dramatist's principal source for the story of the magistrate corrupted by lust was an Italian novella by Cinthio, in which the setting is Innsbruck, but this is changed by Shakespeare to Vienna. Why this change was made we can only speculate: was it simply to place the story in a city which was better known, a royal capital, resembling London more closely than the provincial city of Innsbruck did? However, there never was a Duke of Innsbruck or of Vienna, although the younger brother of the Hapsburg king-emperors usually bore the title Archduke of Austria. Yet the new names which Shakespeare gave his characters are all Italian – Vincentio, Angelo, Claudio, Lucio, Isabella, and so on, and the impression is that this is essentially an Italian play, transferred, as *Twelfth Night* was, out of Italy. It is a darker Italy perhaps than that of the other plays, but the prisons and the brothels are in perfect accord with what we know of the life of late medieval Italian cities – indeed was there any city in Europe without them? If there was some contemporary resonance in the English mind about the name Vienna, it seems impossible now to recover it, and contacts between Elizabethan England and Hapsburg Austria were few.

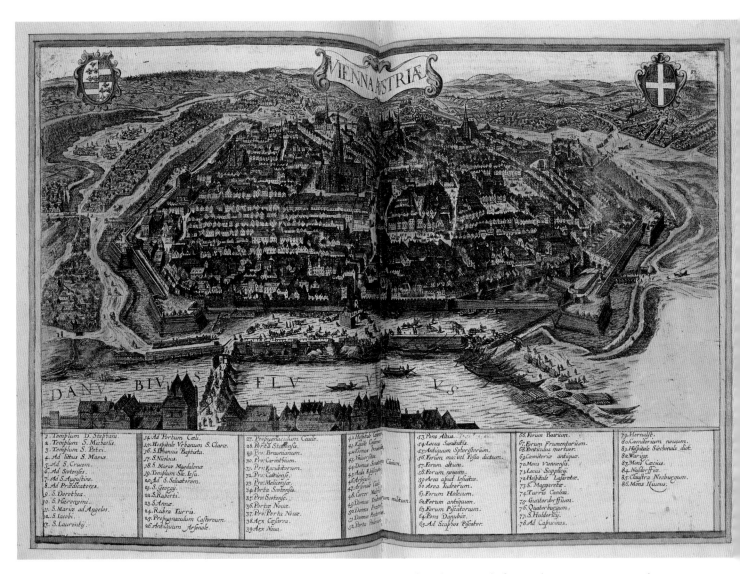

58 Vienna, from Braun and Hogenberg, 1617; the expansion of the city beyond the walls into disreputable suburbs is evident here, as it is in contemporary maps of London.

There are, however, just a few historical facts about Vienna in the sixteenth century which seem strangely relevant to the play. The first is that in 1529 the city had been besieged by the Turks, and had naturally been greatly damaged, especially in the extramural suburbs. After the crisis had passed and the defences were being made good, Archduke Ferdinand I, later to become Emperor, ordered that the suburbs should be pulled down in order to provide a *glacis*, a wide open strip of land around the city to provide a clear field of fire from the rebuilt fortifications. The motive is different, but the idea of deliberately pulling down disorderly houses in the suburbs was part of Angelo's strategy to eradicate vice; Angelo too wanted to create a cordon sanitaire around the city. The second fact is that one of Ferdinand's successors, Rudolf II, abandoned Vienna in the 1570s and shifted his capital to Prague for some thirty years, and Vienna naturally suffered as a consequence of the court's absence. The Duke's departure from Vienna is the opening move in the play's story, leaving power in the hands of Angelo, his deputy. These facts may both be mere coincidence, but we wonder if Shakespeare could have learned of them somehow and used them in planning the structure of the play. Neither is taken from Cinthio's source narrative, where the magistrate is sent to Innsbruck by the Emperor, and where the brothel scenes do not appear. The idea of Vienna as a misplaced part of Italy seems odd, but Hamlet claimed that the murder acted by the players took place in Vienna, 'Gonzago is the duke's name, his wife Baptista',[29] so the link between Vienna and inhabitants with Italian names appears again.

Navarre, the setting of *Love's Labour's Lost*, is at first sight another enigma, compounded by the absence of literary or historical sources, since the story of the intellectual academy which is swiftly transformed into an academy of love is one of the few plays which Shakespeare seems to have invented entirely himself. Navarre was a kingdom mainly on the Spanish side of the Pyrenees whose throne had passed by marriage to the French dynasty of Bourbon. It was annexed to the Spanish Crown in 1515, but the royal house of Navarre retained its status, with Pamplona as its capital. In Elizabethan England, the name Navarre meant only one thing: Henri, King of Navarre since 1572, and the leading Protestant nobleman in France, a country that was being torn apart by religious wars. Henri, aged nineteen, had narrowly escaped death in the massacre of St Bartholomew's Day; he later emerged as a great military leader and heir to the throne of France. Regarded as a hero in England, he was sent forces to aid his struggle, but deep disillusionment followed when in 1593 he abjured his Protestant faith and embraced Catholicism in order to claim the throne. He did this, however, in the interests of France, to bring to an end a religious civil war which had already shed an ocean of blood and which showed no sign of abating. Henri swiftly put an end to the fighting, and reinstated himself in English eyes first by making war on Spain and then by signing the famous

59 (*overleaf*) The entry of Philip IV into Pamplona, *c.*1646, by Juan Bautista Martinez del Mazo: a royal visit to the city like the one which sets in motion the events of *Love's Labour's Lost*.

60 Northern Spain from the Münster Ptolemy atlas of 1540, marking Pamplona and the kingdom of Navarre, although not indicating that Navarre extended into France.

Edict of Nantes proclaiming freedom of conscience to Protestants. Any mention of a King of Navarre in a fictitious context could only evoke the figure of Henri IV, especially since there never was a King Ferdinand of Navarre. The fact that Henri, although a skilled and judicious ruler, was known to be a slave to love, conducting numerous affairs, did him no harm in the popular imagination.

It seems certain therefore that in placing this elegant play about the games of love in the Kingdom of Navarre, Shakespeare was making use of the resonance that Henri IV's name would have, and that the theme of making and breaking vows would give it an added relevance. The fact that historical figures named Biron, de Mayenne and Longueville were all servants or allies of Henri IV, and that their names would have been familiar to many people in England, makes the identification even stronger.

Henri's marriage to Marguerite of Valois had been the occasion for the St
Bartholomew's Day massacre, and the couple had promptly separated, she
being a Catholic. Only six years later did the two royal families of Valois
and Bourbon meet to reunite them, an event which happened at Nérac in
Gascony, where an extended royal party took place, with hunting and other
entertainments. This episode was recorded by Marguerite and published
in 1628, but earlier reports of it may have reached England; if so, it would
provide the final piece of the jigsaw in reconstructing the background to
the play. This is not to argue that *Love's Labour's Lost* is a political allegory,
parody or satire, merely that it explains why Shakespeare might have chosen
the otherwise unfamiliar region of Navarre in which to set this, his only
'Spanish' play.

One final speculation: Henri IV's grandmother was Marguerite of
Navarre (1492–1549), the central figure in a kind of intellectual academy
of writers and scholars, who was herself the author of the *Heptameron*, a
collection of stories in the manner of Boccaccio, on the subject of love,
virtue, honour and wit. Is it possible that her name or her work was familiar
to Shakespeare, and that this too contributed to the image of Navarre as
a place where his academy of learning, love and comedy might take place?
The Navarre setting is admittedly left behind in the two rural songs on
spring and winter which end the play, songs that that are purely English
in spirit.

Two of the non-Italian plays are set in France, and perhaps it comes as a
surprise that one of them is *As You Like It.* This play has long been regarded
as the most English of all the plays, located as it is in the Forest of Arden
only a few miles from Stratford, and offering an idyllic pastoral vision of the
Warwickshire countryside in which Shakespeare grew up. Perhaps it does
offer that vision, but the evidence is there that the true setting is in France.
The play is based directly, but with many changes of detail, on the short
novel *Rosalynde* by Thomas Lodge, published in 1590. Here the Orlando
character is said to be the son of Sir John of Bordeaux, and the Arden
forest to which they all run away is in the direction of Lyons. The names
of the principal characters are strange, and certainly more foreign than
English – Rosader, Saladyne, Torismond and Gerismond – but are they
French? Shakespeare changes these to names that are more recognizably

French, such as Orlando, Oliver, Frederick and Jaques, and adds Charles, Le Beau and Amiens. This forest is inhabited by lions, and perhaps the ancient forest of Ardennes may have been in the sixteenth century, but the Warwickshire Forest of Arden certainly was not. After the marriages that end *Rosalynde*, Lodge tells us that the characters all go to Paris to be feasted by the king, and that Rosader (Orlando) is made Duke of Namurs.

So the most familiar of all Shakespeare's settings, and the one most personal to him, apparently dissolves into a forest out of a romance somewhere in France, not even identifiable as the Ardennes, since that cannot conceivably be described as lying between Bordeaux and Lyons. It is curious that the name Arden does not appear on the map of Warwickshire by Christopher Saxton, one of the series of detailed English county maps published in 1579. Since it was the Saxton maps which served as the cartographic base for the magnificent tapestry maps woven in the 1590s in the workshops of Sheldon, they too fail to mark Arden. The forest is named, however, on the curious maps which illustrated Drayton's topographical epic of England, *Poly-Olbion*, published in 1612. We must wonder what Shakespeare intended his audience to understand by this forest, but he must

61 A section of the Sheldon tapestry map of Warwickshire, *c.*1590, showing its technical craftsmanship and the density of place names, copied entirely from the Saxton maps; strangely, however, the name Arden does not appear on either.

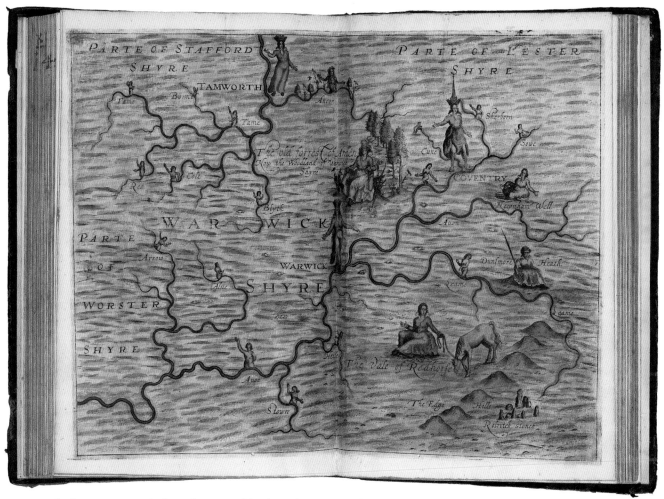

surely have expected that they would identify it with the English Arden, and this identification has become complete in the meta-life that the play has enjoyed for four hundred years.

All's Well That Ends Well has multiple settings, moving from the opening scenes in Count Bertram's home in Roussillon to the king's court in Paris; it then follows a military campaign to Florence, before returning for the dramatic climax to Roussillon. The scenes in Paris are all interiors and there is no sense of a special location; nor is the king named, so that the play is not fixed in time either. The oddity about the Roussillon setting is that the region was, like Navarre, divided geographically and culturally between Spain and France, and Roussillon was far more Spanish than French. Bertram is described as the Count of Roussillon, and not only is he a subject of the King of France, but he is actually the King's ward following his own father's death. The territory of Roussillon was ruled by the house of Aragon, and continued to be so until the mid-seventeenth century when Perpignan and the whole region were formally ceded to France.

62 The Forest of Arden named on the fantasy map of Warwickshire in Drayton's *Poly-Olbion*, 1612.

63 (*above*) An Edenic woodland scene from Münster's *Cosmographia*, 1552, matching the atmosphere of *As You Like It* – whether that woodland is in England or in France.

64 (*opposite*) Manuscript map by Jean Cavalier of the County of Roussillon, 1635. It is orientated from the north-east towards the south-west. Perpignan is clearly visible, but Narbonne is off the map to the east.

This puzzle sends us back to the play's source, one of Boccaccio's stories from *The Decameron*, retold in the English version by William Painter and published in *The Palace of Pleasure* in 1566. But here too the same French–Spanish dichotomy appears. Boccaccio was writing in the 1350s when there was no possible question mark over Roussillon's Spanish identity; perhaps this was purely a lapse of concentration or memory. But strangely there is a similar question about the Florentine scenes too. In the play we are told that Florence, at war with its neighbour Sienna, appealed to the French king for military help, which he officially declined, but still encouraged young French noblemen to go as privateers. Is this war a historical event? Between 1552 and 1555, Cosimo de Medici waged war on Sienna, finally annexing the city to Florence; but again the Florence–Sienna conflict appears in Boccaccio as the pretext on which Bertram seizes for leaving his home after his forced marriage to Helena. Painter wrote that Bertram 'took his journey into Tuscany, where understanding that the Florentines and Senois were at war, he determined to take the Florentines' part, and

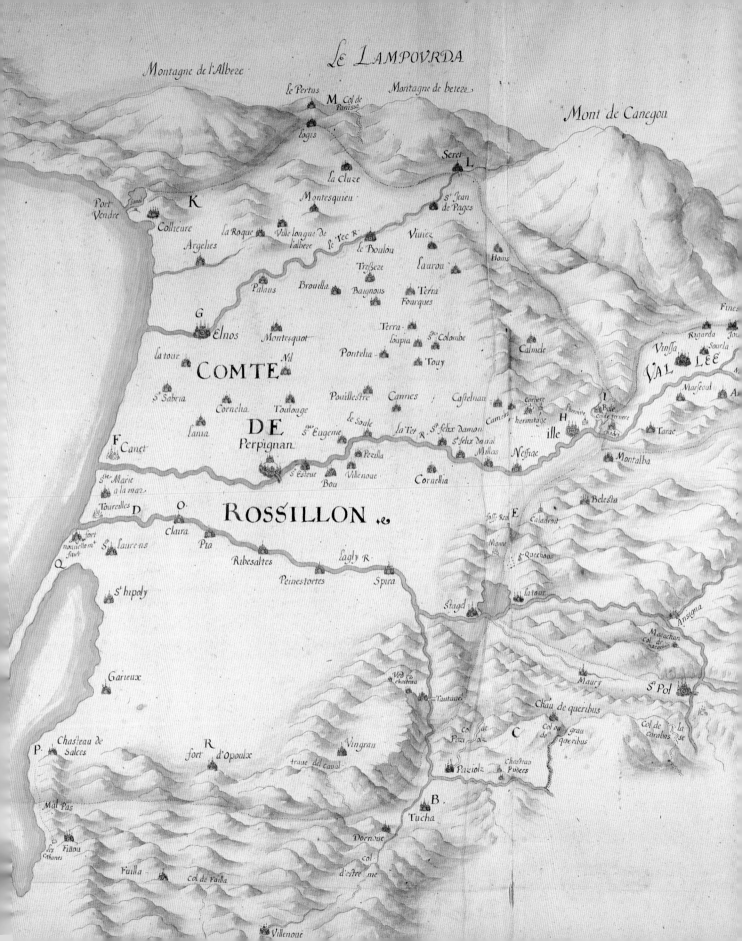

LA RIVIERE DE SEINE

was willingly received'. Painter exactly followed the original here, so either Boccaccio is referring to a much earlier conflict, or he simply invented it. This is another historical oddity that is difficult to explain, since French military intervention in northern Italy did not pre-date 1490.

Does any of this matter in our approach to this complex and intriguing play? Not very much, except that perhaps it demonstrates a little of the way that Shakespeare sometimes worked: the way that the mere outline of a pre-existing story would take hold of his imagination, spurring him to re-create it on a deeper psychological and emotional level, yet caring little or nothing for certain practical details, which he was content to take over verbatim from his sources. This was not always the case, as we saw when he changed the location of *Othello*, *The Taming of the Shrew* or *Measure for Measure*, or when he reinvented a location such as Illyria or Navarre. In these cases he may have had a half-conscious reason – there may have been something in his mind, perhaps based on his reading that prompted these minor artistic decisions. What these factors may have been is almost invariably unknown: with Shakespeare, no matter how much we find out, another mystery always confronts us.

Hamlet's Elsinore is the classic example of a place that has achieved fame in the meta-life of a Shakespeare play, yet it has no real historical connection either with Hamlet or Shakespeare himself. Sixteenth-century Elsinore was a small town on the narrow strait into the Baltic, whose importance was described by Fynes Moryson following his visit there is 1593:

> This is a poor village, but much frequented by seafaring men,
> by reason of the straight sea called the Sound, where the King
> of Denmark hath laid so great impositions upon ships and
> goods coming out of the Baltic Sea or brought into the same, as
> this sole profit passeth all the revenues of his kingdom. In this
> village a strong castle called Croneburg lyeth upon the mouth
> of the straight.[30]

The Kronborg Palace was built between 1574 and 1585 as a magnificent new royal residence, replacing an older medieval fortress. Kronborg became identified as Hamlet's castle, although this was always a historical impossibility. The story of Hamlet first appeared in a medieval Latin chronicle

65 Central section of Merian's panoramic view of Paris, 1650, the classic view from the west. *All's Well* has little sense of Paris as a living location, but the royal scenes must be imagined as taking place at the Louvre Palace.

Pharus

Interior Arcis magnificentia

66 Helsingor (Elsinore) by de Wit, 1660, showing the shipping whose tolls brought wealth to the Danish crown, and the Kronborg Palace which they built. The island of Hven, where Tycho Brahe sited his great observatory, is clearly seen.

FRETI DANICI OR SVNDT ACCVRATISS DELINEATIO.

SEBVRGVM

LANDESKRON

HVENA   Vraniburgum   ELBOGEN

VM   D   AN   IAE   FRETVM   ORR   SVND

EBVRGV

HELSCHENOR   Groseeck

Lundehoue

written by Saxo Grammaticus, which was to Danish history what Geoffrey of Monmouth, the collector of the Arthurian legends, was to British. Its time period was entirely vague but certainly ancient and pre-Christian, and its setting was Jutland rather than Zealand. This story was retold by, among others, the sixteenth-century French author François de Belleforest, and it was in this form that Shakespeare knew it, but Belleforest in his turn still makes no mention of Elsinore. Therefore Shakespeare must have deliberately chosen to relocate the story to the castle at Elsinore, presumably to give the play a ring of contemporary authenticity, a name that audiences would recognize. Between 1570 and 1600, Denmark was to some extent in the news in England. There were protracted and sometimes tense negotiations about the onerous shipping tolls into the Baltic, and in 1589 King James VI of Scotland married Princess Anne of Denmark, daughter of King Frederick II, the man who had built the Kronborg. Since James was virtually certain to be England's next king, there was considerable interest in the idea of a Danish-born queen.

The cliff mentioned in the play – 'that beetles o'er his base into the sea'[31] – is poetic licence, as the coast is flat there, a fact which would have been clear from views of the town published soon after the Kronborg was completed. No one would have cared much about this detail, for if they had been familiar with Belleforest – where there is no ghost urging Hamlet to revenge, no play within a play, no Laertes, and no death of Hamlet – they would have been more interested in the narrative changes that Shakespeare made. However, a decade before the play that we know, another *Hamlet* was staged whose text has not survived and whose author is unknown – it may have been Thomas Kyd, author of *The Spanish Tragedy* – but which is referred to in several contemporary sources. It seems certain that Shakespeare knew this work, that he followed it in some respects, and altered it in others. Today, many of the world's Shakespearean scholars would probably sacrifice several years of their lives for the glory of rediscovering, reading and analysing this lost play, and isolating exactly what Shakespeare's personal contribution really was to the long, complex Hamlet story.

It is a striking fact that *Hamlet* conveys such a strong sense of place, perhaps stronger even than *As You Like It*'s Forest of Arden, when, on

67 The king of Denmark, from Münster's *Cosmographia*, 1552.

factual analysis, it turns out to be so entirely a place of the imagination. Hamlet's castle is the archetypal dark, haunted house from a Gothic tale, looking out over a cold northern sea, a house where passion, treachery, murder, madness and revenge are all equally possible. To us in the post-romantic and post-Freudian age, it has become an image of the dark, subconscious regions of the mind. Out in the sound, only a few miles from Kronborg, is the island of Ven, where, at exactly the same time that Shakespeare was writing *Hamlet*, the great Danish astronomer Tycho Brahe lived and worked in his personal castle, Uraniborg, 'Castle of the Stars'. Tycho revolutionized mankind's understanding of the heavens, yet today, as a tourist destination, Ven is nowhere compared to the attractions of the Kronborg, such is the power of imagination, and the lure of the most famous play in world literature.

68 'And why such daily cast of brazen cannon...' From Münster's *Cosmographia*, 1552.

THREE

British plays,
ancient, medieval
& modern

Shakespeare's England: A sense of place

WHEN CONSIDERING THE plays that have British settings, the question that naturally arises is this: is there a central difference in theme, or feeling or sense of place between the British plays and the European? Should we expect a more personal sense of location – psychological and geographical – to arise from settings in the writer's own country, some of which he may have been personally familiar with? Did the fact of his and his audience's shared national identity bring into focus certain themes which we do not find in the European plays, and perhaps exclude others?

I think the answer is that there is indeed one characteristic theme which unites the British plays and marks them off from the others. These plays, from the legendary era in which *King Lear* takes place, through to the era of the Tudor dynasty represented in *Henry VIII*, all centre, with one exception, on kingship, on the king as the great focal symbol of nationhood; the single exception is *The Merry Wives of Windsor*, a bourgeois comedy. The king is halfway to the gods, powerful but fallible, sometimes magnanimous, sometimes cruel, and the famous words from *Lear*, 'As flies to wanton boys, are we to the gods;/They kill us for their sport',[1] could, in medieval society, be equally true of kings. The assumption that a king will be wise, noble, courageous and honest is tested again and again, and those ideal qualities are measured against his humanity, his frailty, his weakness and his capacity for outright evil. This testing, this historical investigation, is played out against the background of the lives of common people in real

69 *Anglia Figura*, *c.*1538, the manuscript map gifted to Henry VIII. Its purpose was to display the King's realm of Anglia as embracing the whole of the British Isles; the mapping of Ireland and Scotland is much cruder than that of England and Wales.

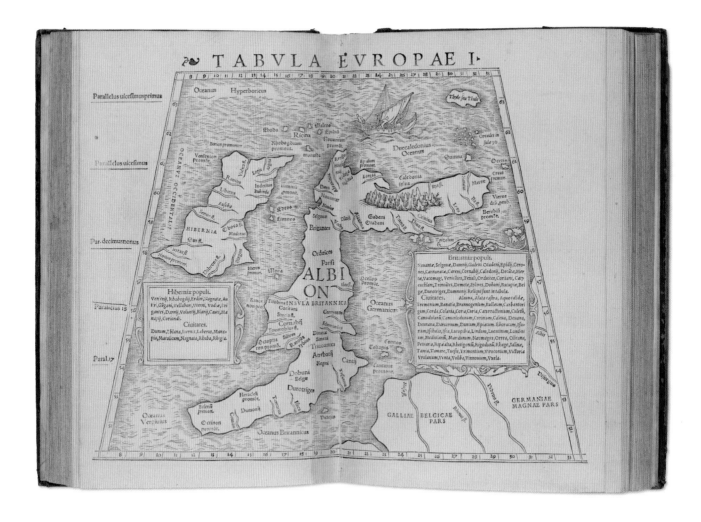

70 Ancient Britain, a Ptolemaic map published by Münster in 1540. With its distorted form, its empty spaces filled by tribal names, the great forest in Scotland and the primitive ship, this seems to evoke the prehistoric land in which *Lear* might have taken place.

places, London principally, but also Yorkshire, Kent, Wales, the Midlands, Scotland and in named towns within all these areas. In these plays, and especially in those which chronicle the Wars of the Roses, we have a sense of movement to and fro across the country, a prolonged struggle in a multitude of locations for the soul of England. The English place names anchor this struggle, this kingly theme, in real space. In the fundamental work of Tudor historiography which Shakespeare used as his prime source, Holinshed's *Chronicles*, published in 1577, we see this theme unmistakably. The history of England is the story of the kings of England: there is no other possible theme which can define that history.

That this struggle is in Shakespeare largely tragic is shown by the fact that all the kings, except Henry V and Henry VIII, end badly, in disillusionment, betrayal or violent death. The message is this: when the king is virtuous the nation thrives in peace and war, but when the king loses touch with the ideals of kingship, then the nation sickens. This personal dissection of royal character explains why all these plays must be in the past: it would have been politically impossible for Shakespeare to have explored this theme by reference to current events, to have portrayed a monarch recognizable in any way as the figure then reigning, or even as being among his or her ancestors. This understanding of kingship and nationhood would have been felt as something personal and English by Shakespeare and his audience; hence it did not emerge in the European plays, including even the Roman plays. Roman leaders like Caesar, Mark Antony, Brutus or Coriolanus, for all their pride and valour, are not shown as possessing this almost mystical unity with the Roman people.

The kings in the British plays interact with their peers, the rebellious nobles, who share with the king the power to make history. But we are also shown the underside of life, the common people, in Falstaff and his cronies, in Jack Cade, Dick the Butcher and the mob of peasants, and in assorted characters like Justice Shallow, Mouldy, Bullcalf, Poor Tom, and various servants, fools, porters and murderers – the people who endure history. The official picture of England's uniqueness is given in John of Gaunt's celebrated speech in *Richard II*:

> This royal throne of kings, this sceptred isle,
> This earth of majesty, this seat of Mars,
> This other Eden, demi-paradise;
> This fortress built by Nature for herself
> Against infection and the hand of war;
> This happy breed of men, this little world;
> This precious stone set in the silver sea ...
> ... This blessed plot, this earth, this realm, this England,
> This nurse, this teeming womb of royal kings,
> Feared by their breed and famous by their birth...[2]

This is poetry written in praise of a royal land defined by its history, but the reverse side is precisely the struggle that rages ceaselessly around the throne, a struggle whose grim effects are laid bare by Henry VI when he laments: 'O bloody times! / Whiles lions war and battle for their dens / Poor harmless lambs abide their enmity.'[3]

Gaunt's idea that Britain's island status will protect her from 'the hand of war' becomes highly ironic in view of the fact that war comes from within, that the events of *Richard II* create the conditions for the destructive Wars of the Roses. But the idea of the rock-like fortress, the precious gem islanded in the midst of the sea, had become very topical and very appealing in the age of the Elizabethan seafarers, and in the aftermath of the Spanish Armada's defeat. The Saxton maps – those of the coastal counties and his great wall map of the whole country – abound in images of Neptune, of sea-monsters, and of fighting ships. There is in fact such a visually descriptive feel to Gaunt's speech that it seems possible that Shakespeare was recalling these maps in his mind's eye when he penned it, or even had a map in front of him. The foundation work of English topography, William Camden's *Britannia*, was published in 1586, and its title page also displays the island nation between Neptune and Ceres, the gods of sea and earth. When we read the extended, repetitive, confusing textual descriptions of England's geography in Holinshed's historical chronicle, first published in 1577 – the prose listing of endless capes, bays, rivers, hills, towns and cities – we understand the pressing need for the Saxton maps which appeared two years later, in 1579, maps which gave a clear visual image of the land, which the eye could interpret instantly.

Away from the coasts and the battlefields, there is another kind of poetry that is strikingly absent from the British plays, namely the poetry of love, which apparently blossomed only in the sun of southern Europe. The one British play which is in any sense about love, *The Merry Wives of Windsor*, is a satirical portrait of an ageing rogue, behind whose mask of seductive lovemaking lies a certain measure of lust, but an even greater measure of greed. Likewise the fantastic inner and outer transformations that fill the love-comedies like *All's Well*, *Much Ado*, *The Shrew* and *Twelfth Night* have an exotic, magical feel – which was perhaps Shakespeare's tribute to his beloved Ovid – which belongs only to southern Europe, and which simply could not be squared with a setting in the audience's real world of London or Windsor or Yorkshire.

Along with the love theme, the love songs have vanished from the British plays. *Cymbeline* has the mysterious funeral incantation 'Fear no more the heat o' the sun', while *Henry VIII* has the magical song in praise of music, 'Orpheus with his lute', but these are different in kind from 'O mistress mine', or 'Take, O take those lips away', – they are less personal, more serious and more literary. Of all the songs, the most truly evocative of rural England, an England shivering in its winter garments, has been strangely transferred to the Navarre of *Love's Labour's Lost*:

> When icicles hang by the wall,
> And Dick the shepherd blows his nail,
> And Tom bears logs into the hall,
> And milk comes frozen home in pail,
> When blood is nipp'd and ways be foul,
> Then nightly sings the staring owl ...[4]

There is in fact a certain level of narrative detail tied to specific place names, which we find in the British plays, but would scarcely expect in the European. Think of Windsor, and Falstaff tipped into the Thames at Datchet; think of *Lear*, and the samphire gatherers on the cliffs above Dover; think of Cade commanding his rebels to storm 'up Fish Street and down St Magnus corner',[5] and kill whomsoever they meet; think of Richard III asking the Bishop of Ely for strawberries which he had seen in his garden at Holborn; think of Richard again, receiving like blow after blow the news that his enemy, the Earl of Richmond, is landing at Milford Haven, while rebels are arming in Devonshire, in Kent and in Yorkshire, conjuring up a picture of a power-base that is crumbling all over England; think of Henry VI's fearsome queen, Margaret of Anjou, welcoming her timid husband to the town of York with the sight of the Duke of York's head spiked over the city gate; think of Falstaff cursing Poins by saying his wit is as thick as Tewkesbury mustard; think of Poins planning the celebrated robbery outside Rochester with the words 'early at Gadshill there are pilgrims going to Canterbury with rich offerings, and traders riding to London with fat purses.'[6] All these details are based on familiarity with certain place names, with a knowledge of location that the actors share with the audience.

71 A court fool of the sixteenth century, despised and privileged in equal measure, from Münster's *Cosmographia*, 1552.

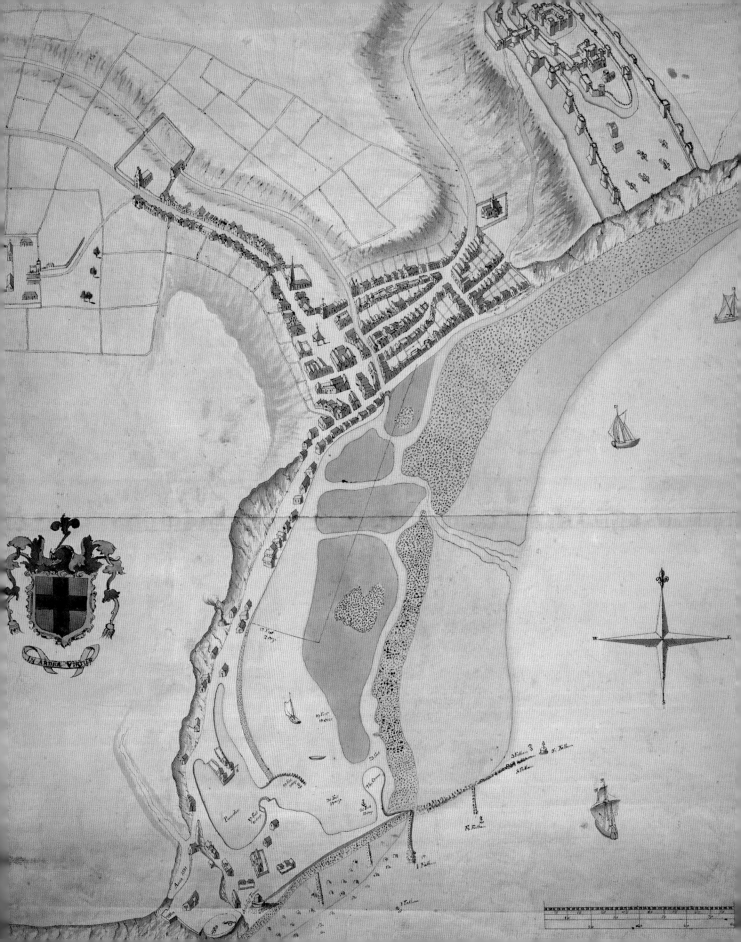

IN ARDEA VIRTUS

The ancient &
medieval plays

K ING LEAR is the most elusive British play to pin down in time
or place. We never learn where Lear's palace stands, the setting
of the crucial opening scene, nor where Gloucester's castle is – it
seems to be in the midst of a bleak heathland. If Gloucester's two sons
live with him there, why should Edgar need to write him a secret and
self-incriminating letter? Dover is the only identifiable location in the
main story, the natural point of contact between England and France,
but why does Gloucester need to travel to Dover in order to kill himself?
The dukes of Albany and Cornwall play major roles, but their lands
and people remain always unseen in the background, not surprisingly
perhaps in the case of Albany, which was the extreme northern region
of Scotland.

The story of Lear, the king who divides his kingdom among his
daughters and so precipitates personal and political crises, first appears in
the medieval chronicle of Geoffrey of Monmouth, composed in the twelfth
century. Lear is said to be the tenth British king after Brut, the legendary
founder of the nation, an exile after the fall of Troy. In Geoffrey's scheme,
Lear lived about the time of the prophet Isaiah and of the founding of
Rome by Romulus and Remus. Geoffrey makes him the founder of a
town on the River Soar called Kaerleir, known in Saxon as Leicester. In
his *Chronicles of England, Scotland and Ireland*, published in 1577, and
Shakespeare's indispensable guide to British history, Ralph Holinshed is
quite specific that Lear began his reign 3,105 years after the creation of the

72 Manuscript map of Dover
by Thomas Digges, 1581, the
one clearly identified location
in *King Lear*. This drawing was
preparatory to the building of
a new harbour, to replace the
small one here located at the
western edge of the town.

world, an event traditionally dated at 4004 BCE. So we are in approximately the year 900 BCE, to us an age in British history that long pre-dated any historical record and was therefore purely legendary, but not so to the Elizabethans. Holinshed follows Geoffrey in the story of Cordelia's removal to France, and her subsequent return to England to reinstate Lear to the throne. Lear died a natural death and was buried at Leicester, following which Cordelia's nephews usurped her throne and Cordelia took her own life in prison. Shakespeare took the story of Gloucester and his son from a separate source, and blended it with the royal narrative. As has often been remarked, in this ancient setting Lear naturally lived in a pre-Christian, pagan world, swearing by Apollo and the more sinister Hecate, a deity of magic and witchcraft.

By common consent *King Lear* is the most violent of Shakespeare's plays, with a violence of mind, of spirit and not merely of the body, a violence that is mirrored in nature's storms. Lear's impetuous lack of judgement and still more his madness are all the more terrible in a king, for it is he who triggers the events which shatter the peace of the kingdom and harmony of the cosmos. Shakespeare seems here to be drawing on the very ancient and widespread belief that the king is an intermediary between mankind and the gods. The king's wisdom and rectitude guarantee cosmic peace, while his transgressions may bring chaos and suffering to his people. This is a drama that takes place in an indefinable region of myth rather than the real historic kingdom of England, but it is interesting to see the theme of kingship taking centre stage once again, in such a totally different context from that of the later Wars of the Roses plays.

The second play set in ancient Britain is *Cymbeline*, a late romance filled with fantastic incidents and sharply contrasting themes and settings, which make it one of the strangest and most difficult plays to grasp and assess. The shifts in place are sudden and radical – from Cymbeline's British court to Rome, to the Welsh mountains, to a battlefield, a prison, a dream-world seen in a vision, and finally back to the court. Yet paradoxically this rich, baffling phantasmagoria is, unlike *Lear*, quite securely anchored in history. The model for Cymbeline is known by his Latin name Cunobelinus, who lived shortly after Caesar's invasion of Britain, ruling for thirty-five years from 33 BCE onwards; thus he was king of at

73 A mosaic of a Romano-British lady of the fourth century; in our imagination this could stand as a portrait of Imogen in *Cymbeline*.

least part of Britain at the time of Christ's birth, a fact which appealed to the old chroniclers. He is called *Rex Brittonum* on his silver coins, several examples of which have been found, including one which states that Cunobelinus had been nurtured in Rome under Caesar's care. In his *Chronicles*, Holinshed writes that Augustus freed him from the tribute money required by Rome, but later, possibly in the following reign, payment was demanded again, and a Roman force was sent to enforce it, which was however defeated by the Britons. These events are exactly as presented in the play, where the king's two sons are faithfully named as Arviragus and Guiderius, although the story of their abduction as children was Shakespeare's own invention.

As with Lear, the location of the royal palace is not given, but, since we are firmly in Roman Britain, London is the most likely guess, and London is mentioned in passing as 'Lud's-town' in the play. But in *Cymbeline*, as still more in Shakespeare's next play, *The Winter's Tale*, he sets up a dichotomy between the false, malevolent world of the court and the noble simplicity of the countryside, or in this case the rugged beauty of the Welsh mountains and forests. Here the lost princes' guardian, Belarius, teaches them to live in honest freedom, honouring the sun and the heavens instead of corrupt earthly rulers. Here the king's two sons have been nurtured in secret, but, as in so many fairy stories, their royal character shines through their humble dress and mean surroundings. So again we see the theme of kingship, its corruption and possible redemption through new generations of royal blood. Cymbeline is, like Lear, rash and poor in judgement, and he too rejects his daughter. He too sees his kingdom threatened, but his throne is saved by the actions of his two sons, whose true identity is then revealed to him. From this wild, northern, fairy-tale world, we are briefly transported to Rome itself for the character of Iachimo and the fidelity-wager story, but it is a Rome that feels more like that of the Renaissance than of Augustus' time, and indeed Shakespeare took the story directly from a Boccaccio novella, and added it as one more surprising element to this complex romance.

The scene chosen for the confrontation between Romans and Britons is Milford Haven. If we wonder why, Camden's *Britannia* seems to provide the answer:

74 (*above*) Coins of King Cymbeline illustrated in Camden's *Britannia*, 1607.

At length the land shrinketh back on both sides, giving place unto the sea, which encroaching upon it a great way, maketh the haven which Englishmen call Milford Haven, than which there is not another in all Europe more noble or safer, such variety it hath of nooked bays and so many coves and creeks for harbour of ships, wherewith the banks are on every side indented, that I may use the poet's words:

> The sea, disarmed here of winds, within high bank and hill
> Enclosed is, and learns thereby to be both calm and still.

Neither is this haven famous for the secure safeness thereof more than for the arrival therein of King Henry VII, a prince of most happy memory, who from hence gave forth unto England then hopeless, the first signal to hope well and raise itself up, when as it had now long languished in civil miseries and domestical calamities.[7]

This must surely have been the reason that Shakespeare chose Milford Haven – the place where Henry Tudor landed to open his campaign against Richard III, and therefore a place of symbolic importance in the founding of the Tudor dynasty. The Pembrokeshire coast is not mentioned in any of the historical sources as the scene of this ancient battle. An earlier naval victory over the Romans, presumably Caesar's second landing in 54 BCE, is recalled in the play in terms which set up unmistakable echoes of the defeat of the Spanish Armada. After describing Britain rather quaintly as 'Neptune's park, ribbed and paled in / With rocks unscaleable and roaring waters.'[8] Caesar's fleet is said to have been carried 'From off our coast, twice beaten; and his shipping – / Poor ignorant baubles – on our terrible seas, / Like egg-shells moved upon their surges, cracked / As easily 'gainst our rocks.'[9]

It was a victory which made London bright with rejoicing fires, and this is language that would have delighted John of Gaunt, and inspired artists and map-makers to create their images of 'Neptune's park'. With its emphasis on the role of sea storms in the defence of Britain, these lines feel like a reference to an event much nearer to Shakespeare's time, namely the defeat of the Spanish Armada, which was by far the greatest military event to occur during the dramatist's early life. *Cymbeline* is a puzzling, fantasy-romance, crossing boundaries of geography, time and literary genres, challenging us to suspend disbelief and follow in our imagination

75 Roman and British figures illustrated by Braun and Hogenberg, 1575.

the outworking of the reconciliation theme that was the great subject of Shakespeare's final plays.

If we attempt for a moment to align Shakespeare's imaginative world with the historical world, we find that almost a thousand years of shadowy history are claimed to have passed between *King Lear* and *Cymbeline*, and that the same period again passes between *Cymbeline* and *Macbeth*. Yet the theme is still the same: kingship which separates itself from rationality, from moral law or spiritual integrity, bringing disorder, or even chaos to the kingdom. In *Macbeth* moral disintegration takes the radical form of cooperation and conspiracy with demonic powers. This is perhaps seen as the more plausible for taking place in a wild northern kingdom, unfamiliar and remote from the everyday experience of a London audience.

The story of Macbeth was recorded in a multitude of medieval sources, beginning some two hundred years after the events they describe. Perhaps the most surprising single fact that we discover is that Macbeth reigned for seventeen years, from 1040 to 1057, whereas the sense that we get from the play is that the violent events occupy a matter of a few months at most. The real Macbeth killed Duncan openly in battle, he was regarded as the legitimate king, and was secure enough to leave Scotland and make a pilgrimage to Rome. One of the earliest sources, written by Andrew of Wyntoun, gives an intriguing account of the three witches – indicating that they appeared to Macbeth in a dream, not in reality. If this has any authenticity, it suggests that the witches later became externalized, from a mere dream-image into real figures. But Andrew also says that Macbeth himself was of supernatural parentage, that his mother had met a demonic figure in a wood who fathered a child on her. Because of this magical origin, it is Macbeth himself, according to Andrew, who cannot be harmed by any man born of woman, not his enemy Macduff. In Andrew's narrative there is no Lady Macbeth.

The various sources of this kind were drawn together by Holinshed in his *Chronicles* into an account that provided ample material for Shakespeare's imagination to work on. Much can also be made of the play's contemporary relevance to the accession of James I, the first Scottish king of England, with his well-known interest in witchcraft, a subject on which he was an expert and wrote a learned treatise. James was far from popular in England,

Britannus

Romanus

Saxo

Danus

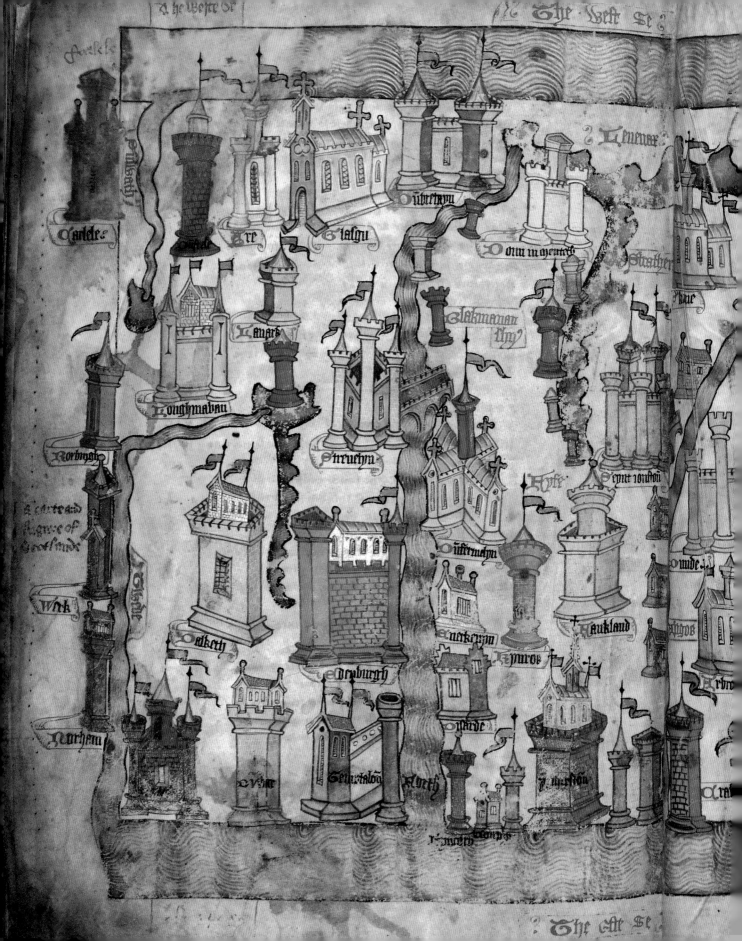

Lenener

Carlele

Castele

Are

Glalgu

Dubreton

Ouin in oyenteth

Strather

Lanark

Blakmanan Tny

Konginnabau

Struelyn

Norbnigh

A carte and figure of Scotlande

Wirk

Ediketh

Dubirmelyn

Kyfe

Sprit ionbou

Aukland

Kynros

Norhem

dephurgh

Selnirtaloun

Korth

thersion

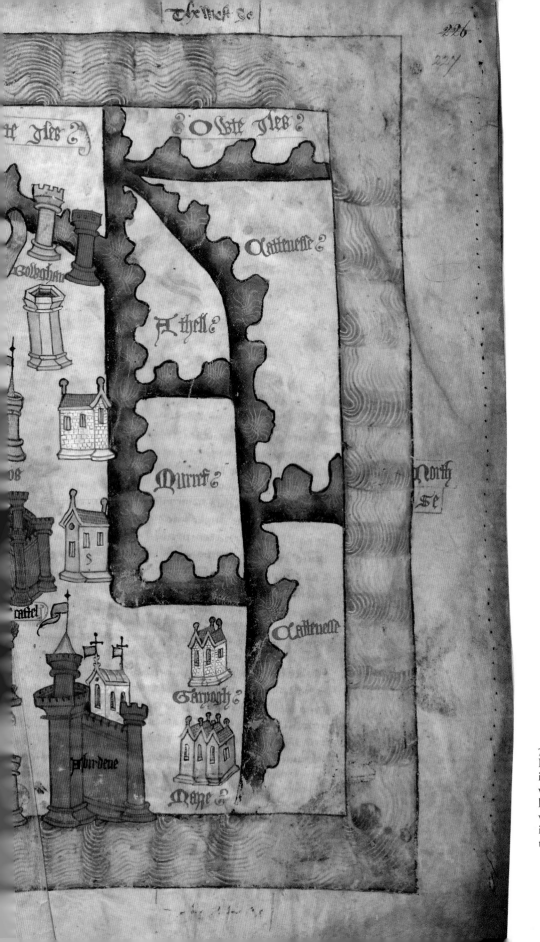

Owte Iles

Catteuesse

Athell

Murref

Golbghau

North
se

cattel

Savagh

Catteuesse

arbir deue

Maze

76 Map of Scotland by John
Harding, 1457, drawn to
illustrate a historical-political
work; topography is non-existent
here – this is a land of castles,
with several place names found
in *Macbeth*; west is at the top of
the map.

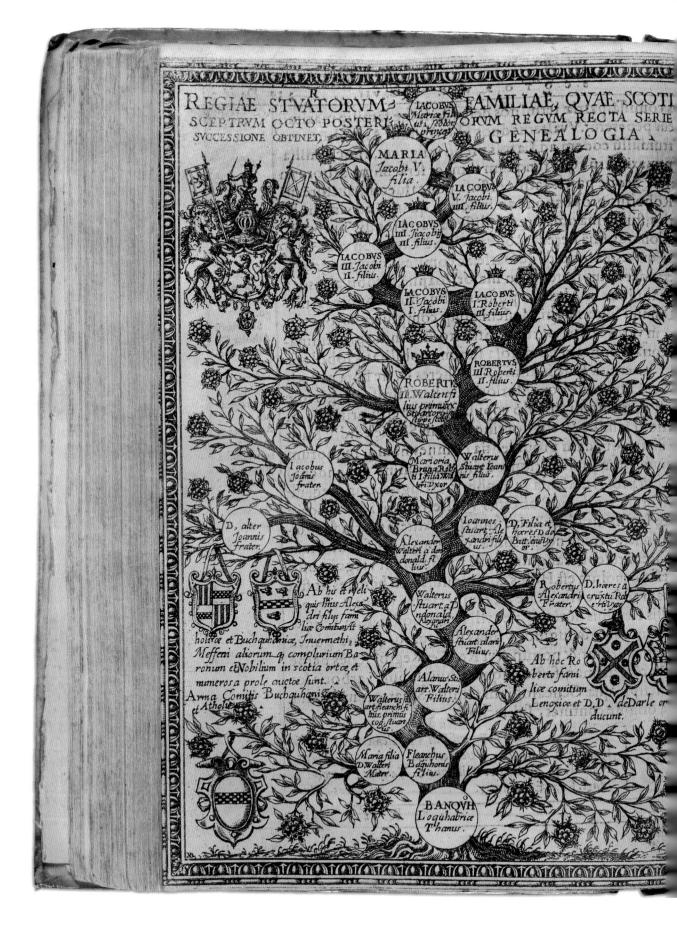

and in 1606, when the play was written, he had just escaped an assassination attempt – the Gunpowder Plot – so that the themes of legitimacy, conspiracy and rebellion were very much in the air. By Holinshed's time, the story of Banquo and his son Fleance had been invented in response to the need to extend the Stuart dynasty's obscure lineage back in time to the Middle Ages. In 1578 a genealogical tree was published tracing the line of descent from Banquo to Mary Queen of Scots and her son, the future King James I. Shakespeare may well have seen this diagram, for he uses the words 'tree', 'root' and 'line' when describing Macbeth's vision of the future kings of Scotland.

The action is centred mainly on Fife and north of the Tay in Perth and Angus. But the geography of Scotland would have been very vague to most Englishmen, since neither Saxton nor Speed, nor indeed anyone else, had mapped Scotland as they had England. General maps of the whole country would of course show cities like Edinburgh, Stirling and St Andrews, with the Forth and the Tay, and the regions that corresponded to counties, such as Fife, Ross and Caithness, which were also the titles of noblemen in the play. However, the now-famous place names from *Macbeth* like Glamis, Cawdor and Dunsinane would at first have conveyed nothing, nor possessed any identity. Yet they undoubtedly created a weird verbal music which would have intensified the sense of exotic location, especially if linked with the mysterious title of 'Thane'. Scone, only a few miles from Perth, was another matter, for it was known as the place of coronation for the kings of Scotland since time immemorial, a place ancient and hallowed by tradition. The Stone of Scone was carried off by Edward I and installed in Westminster, as a symbol that the king of England would henceforth be the king of Scotland. This of course was neatly reversed when James VI and I was crowned as the dual lord of both kingdoms. In 1651, Charles II would be crowned at Scone, before moving south on his unsuccessful campaign against the Parliamentary army.

Of Macbeth, Holinshed remarked rather quaintly that he was 'A valiant gentleman, and one that, if he had not been somewhat cruel of nature, might have been thought most worthy the government of the realm.'[10] There are good

77 (*opposite*) Family tree of King James I, going back to Banquo and Fleance; the personal interest which *Macbeth* may have held for the king has often been analysed. From John Leslie's *De Origine... Scotorum*, 1578.

78 (*below*) A sorceress kneels before a demon she has conjured, from Münster's *Cosmographia*, 1552.

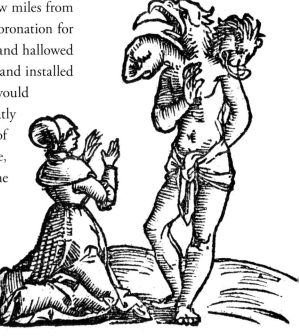

79 Macbeth encounters the three witches, from Holinshed's *Chronicles*, 1587; Holinshed described them as strange and wondrous, not as hideous or as witches.

reasons to suppose that the Macbeth of the play was very different from the Macbeth of history, but it is undoubtedly the former who placed Scotland firmly on the map that we carry in our imagination, so that Dunsinane and Birnam Wood are familiar names to millions who have no idea of their real physical location.

King John is one of the most difficult of Shakespeare's plays to grasp. The action is very complicated, politically and geographically, and the psychological and dramatic forces which should hold the play together are far less evident than we expect from Shakespeare. It is essential to remember that John was king not only of England but of a large part of France too, through his Norman inheritance and through the legacy of his mother, Eleanor of Aquitaine. At various times in the play, John is in conflict with the nobles in both countries, and they in turn are in conflict with each other. In the early and middle scenes, John is making war on rebellious parts of Anjou, while in the final act a French army invades England.

The siege of Angers and its sequel occupy acts 2 and 3, but since King John travelled frequently between England and France, usually for warlike purposes, it is not clear exactly what events are being dramatized. Angers was the capital of the old kingdom of Anjou, noted for its city walls and massive fortified chateau, from where the citizens listen to John's claim to be accepted as the legitimate king after the death of his brother, Richard the Lionheart. John would return to Angers in the course of later conflicts, and Holinshed writes that he

> Did go to assault the gates, which enterprise with fire and sword he so manfully executed that the gates being in a moment broken open, the city was entered and delivered to the soldiers as a prey. So that of the citizens some were taken, some killed, and the walls of the city beaten flat. This done, he went abroad into the country and put all things that were in his way to the like destruction.[11]

80 Miniature of King John on horseback, the nearest thing known to a contemporary portrait of the unpopular monarch. Copied from a contemporary manuscript.

81 An anonymous seventeenth-century drawing of Angers, celebrated for its fortifications; at the top is the massive castle which figures in *King John*.

Holinshed's opinion of the unattractive features of John's character is evident when he tells how, within a few short years,

> King John remembering himself of the destruction of Angers which he had before time greatly loved, began now to repent him that he had destroyed it, and therefore with all speed he took order to have it again repaired, which was done in most beautiful wise, to his great cost and expense. ... But what will not an ordinary man do in the full tide of his fury, much more princes and great men, whose anger is resembled to the roaring of a lion, even upon light occasion oftentimes, to satisfy their unbridled and brainsick affections, which carry them with a swift and full stream into such follies and dotages as are undecent for their degree.[12]

In human terms, the episode which most people remember from *King John* is that of Prince Arthur and his fate, first threatened with blinding

at the hands of Hubert de Burgh, then killed falling from the castle walls. As the son of Geoffrey of Brittany, the deceased elder brother of John, Arthur had legally a stronger claim to the throne than John himself, and was therefore kept imprisoned, finally meeting a highly suspicious end. The historical sources place these events in France, but the play transfers them to England, to Northampton Castle, so that Arthur's dying words are 'Heaven take my soul, and England keep my bones.'[13] Whether John was guilty of Arthur's death or not, this is the turning point of the play, after which John is hated, isolated and powerless, drifting towards his own end. The circumstances of John's death attracted various stories and legends: Shakespeare follows the most familiar one, showing him succumbing to a fever at the Abbey of Swinstead in the East Anglian fens, where he was manoeuvring against the invading French. But the dramatist endorses the rumour that the real cause was poisoning by a monk, because John's policies had for years restricted the freedom of the Church and had diverted its revenues into his own pocket.

King John is detached in time from the other English royal plays, preceding *Richard II* by almost two centuries, but the important theme of conflict in the French territories is introduced. France was both English and not English, English by right and yet it had still to be fought for, and as such it provided a theatre where English nobles and soldiers might display their strength and valour, and their caste superiority. The other all-important theme was the problem of the Crown's legitimacy. The king was supreme and all but sacred – this was not disputed. But who was the true king? If a king were weak, dishonourable, cruel or unjust, might he be removed, and if so how? Not by popular rebellion, by mere force, but by process, by finding a rival king with a better claim to royal descent. This was the strategy that would lie behind all the dynastic wars of the fifteenth century, and drive the action of Shakespeare's later history plays.

The plays of dynastic conflict

IN THE EIGHT PLAYS beginning with *Richard II* and ending with *Richard III*, Shakespeare presented a coherent dramatized account of English royal history covering the century from 1385 to 1485. The purpose of these plays is focused almost exclusively on the theme of kingship, although Falstaff's anarchic comedy towers over the two plays in which he appears. The plays were not, however, written in their historical order, but fall into two groups. The first group comprises the three parts of *Henry VI* and *Richard III*, the last being so organically linked with the others that the whole can be thought of as a tetralogy, whose subject is the Wars of the Roses. The second group goes back in time to show the dynastic conflict that sowed the seeds of that war, so that *Richard II*, the two parts of *Henry IV*, and *Henry V* can again be seen as forming a tetralogy. We cannot say for certain that Shakespeare consciously wrote the second group in order to explain the background of the first, but that is effectively what they do. They do more of course: they give us a tremendous panorama of social and personal conflict raging around and within the person of the king, and a picture of the nation observing and being drawn into that conflict. They move in a rhythm of discontent, hostility, armed battle, temporary truce, followed by bitterness, then the wounds open again and the cycle is replayed once more.

In composing this extended sequence, Shakespeare gave lasting expression to what has been termed the Tudor myth, the belief that the accession of Henry Tudor as King Henry VII finally healed the dynastic conflict

83 Miniature of Richard II presiding over a tournament, exactly as he does in Act 1 of the play. Copied from a contemporary manuscript.

that had dragged on for almost a century and caused immense suffering to the nation. It is called a myth not because it is false or illusory, although it may be that, but because it functioned as a belief: in people's minds it gave shape and meaning to that era of history. Shakespeare is not claimed to be the inventor of this myth, for it was commonplace among Tudor historians, and it lay behind the personality cult which glorified Henry VIII and Queen Elizabeth I. But Tudor historians were not exactly popular and familiar figures after the age of the Tudors had ended, and it was through Shakespeare's plays that this myth was carried down the centuries. A classic expression of the myth is to be found in the very opening words of Edward Hall's great book, *The Union of the Two Noble and Illustre Families of Lancastre and York*, first published in 1548:

What mischief hath insurged in realms by intestine division,
what depopulation hath ensued in countries by civil dissension,
what detestable murder hath been committed in cities by
separate factions, and what calamity hath ensued in famous
regions by domestical discord and unnatural controversy: Rome
hath felt, Italy can testify, France can bear witness, Scotland
may write, Denmark can show, and especially this noble realm
of England can apparently declare and make demonstration.
But what misery, what murder, what execrable plagues this
famous region hath suffered by the division and dissension of
the renowned houses of Lancastre and York, my wit cannot
comprehend nor my tongue declare neither yet my pen fully set
forth. For what noble man living at this day, or what gentleman
of any ancient stock or progeny is there whose lineage hath not
been infested and plagued with this unnatural division? … But
the old divided controversy between the forenamed families of
Lancastre and York, by the union of matrimony celebrate and
consummate between the high and mighty Prince Henry VII

84 The confrontation at Flint
Castle between Richard II in
the centre and Bolingbroke
kneeling, where the king
accepts the inevitability of his
loss of power; copied from a
contemporary manuscript.

85 The scene in Westminster Hall when King Richard abdicates in favour of Bolingbroke; the latter reaches forward for the crown, which Richard is plainly reluctant to hand over; copied from a contemporary manuscript.

and the Lady Elizabeth his most worthy Queen, the one being indubitate heir of the house of Lancastre and the other of York, was suspended and appalled in the person of their most noble, puissant and mighty heir King Henry VIII, and by him clearly buried and perpetually extinct. So that all men more clearly than the sun may apparently perceive that, as by discord great things decay and fall to ruin, so the same by concord be revived and erected. In like wise all regions which by division and dissension be vexed, molested and troubled, be by union and agreement relieved, pacified and enriched.[14]

This in a nutshell is the Tudor myth, and the heaped-up rhetoric of discord and death is an essential part of the myth. This is an introductory preamble which does not yet begin to apportion blame, but it is noticeable that the writer is at pains to show this destructive conflict around the throne as reaching out into the whole nation. The king was always dependent on his aristocratic allies to support his legitimacy, and they in turn called on their feudal dependants and on mercenaries to take up arms in their chosen cause, so the conflict extends in a series of waves which overwhelm countless people and places.

Throughout these plays, the events and their locations in England and in France are inextricably linked in the chronicle sources and in the plays. The conquest of France by Henry V is the culmination of the first group of plays, and its loss is a crucial factor in the second. The names of the cities, battles and castles – Flint, Pomfret, Shrewsbury, Harfleur, Agincourt, Orleans, Towton, Tewksbury, Bosworth and the rest – are landmarks in the political and psychological history the unfolding of which we are watching.

Geographically the plays show an identifiable rhythmic pulse – that between London and the provinces in which the nobles on either side had their local power bases. Most of the encounters and confrontations between the leading players take place in London. The king's palace is not named, but in the fifteenth century this usually meant the Tower, for Greenwich, Hampton Court and Whitehall were not yet built; Richmond was a possibility, and was a favourite place of Richard II. Windsor was a day's journey from London and features infrequently. In addition to the Tower, there were the houses or palaces of the royal dukes, nobles and bishops, many of them lying in the districts between the city and Westminster, and often facing directly onto the river, houses such as Baynards Castle, the Savoy Palace, Arundel House, York House, Durham House and others. Many of the meetings and angry wars of words between king and nobles take place in these now vanished houses, but from them the effects spread out across England, so that the battles are fought not in London but in the country at large, from Hertfordshire to Northumberland, from East Anglia to mid-Wales; in terms of physical violence, southern England and the West Country were largely unaffected.

In the maps of Shakespeare's time, one significant point is worth notic-
ing: the Saxton county maps are very elegantly designed – some are even
beautiful – but they did not include any graphic panels or visual motifs
on the body of the map itself; but when John Speed published his atlas
of county maps in 1611, many of them carried panels containing historical
texts and pictures specifically relating to the Wars of the Roses. Battlefields
like Shrewsbury, Tewkesbury and St Albans are depicted in small, crude
vignettes, while one of the maps – Lancashire – includes a line of portraits
of all the kings involved in the conflict, from Henry IV to Richard III,
representing the opposing houses of York and Lancaster. What had changed
between 1579 and 1611 to suggest this idea to Speed's mind? Could it have
been the impact of Shakespeare's historical plays which made it seem attractive to use these new maps to highlight the landmarks of the wars? By
1611 the Wars of the Roses had been over for 125 years, and cartographically
Speed's maps were directly based on Saxton's, so Speed must surely have
had some specific reason for making these notable additions to their basic
design.

London was the natural – we might almost say the spiritual – centre
of these historical dramas, and it was also the essential catalyst of Shakespeare's life and art. Whatever the outward circumstances of his life might
have been, Shakespeare would probably have matured into a poet, perhaps
a major one; but without the theatres, the competing companies of players,
and the audiences which London alone could provide, he could not have
become the dramatist that we know. London was the place which brought
together the royal court, with its desperate political conflicts, its love
intrigues, the endless struggles for position, the shadow of the Tower with
its threat of judicial murder, the taverns, the brothels, the coarse working
men of the city, and the half-witted beggars; all these merge in our imagination to form a picture of the world which Shakespearean drama inhabits.

Shakespeare's London was not one city, but two: the ancient community
of London, the square mile, squeezed tightly within its encircling walls, and
then, a mile to the west, the royal power-centre of Westminster. Between
the two stretched the highway known as the Strand, its southern side lined
with the great houses of the aristocracy. London was far larger and more
densely populated than Westminster, but the story of London's future

development would be one of relentless westward movement, social and economic, a pull away from the merchants and tradesmen, and towards the court and the government, and the far richer social life they engendered. The city itself was compact, more like an overgrown, swarming village than a modern metropolis. There was only one bridge, on the gates of which the spiked heads of traitors were displayed. The city's Roman-medieval walls were still intact, still fulfilling their ancient role of defence and defining the city's bounds; the seven gates which pierced these walls were locked at night.

Virtually all the houses were of timber, with the characteristic overhang in the upper stories; these were the houses swept away in the Great Fire of 1666. So too was old St Paul's Cathedral, a Gothic building whose spire had collapsed in 1561 when it was struck by lightning. The population in 1585, when Shakespeare arrived in the city, is thought to have been around 150,000. Even when the plague was dormant, London was a place of death, for the mortality rate in the city was horrifying, always exceeding the birth rate, and yet the population continued to grow, fed by immigration from the towns and countryside of England and from the continent, especially the persecuted Protestants from France and the Netherlands; Shakespeare himself was one such immigrant, and he mixed with many others. Death was grotesquely evident in another sense – in the executions that took place regularly at Tyburn, Smithfield, Tower Hill or Lincoln's Inn Fields, where criminals and especially traitors were publicly butchered, always outside the city's boundaries as if to distance the horror, necessary as it was, from civilized society. These bloody scenes undoubtedly acted as ritual expressions of social and political law, and the merciless vengeance which society would take on transgressors.

The city was self-governing, under its mayor and court of aldermen, but in the last resort it could not defend itself against a physical attack from outside, for example in the Peasants' Revolt of 1381 or the 1450 rebellion led by Jack Cade, which features in part II of *Henry VI*. The city's great source of strength was its ability to raise money, not least for the Crown. This relationship went back to the Crusade of Richard the Lionheart, and all monarchs until the end of the seventeenth century would continue to deal directly with the money men of London. Jews

86 (*overleaf*) Braun and Hogenberg's map of London, 1572. The first printed map of the city has become the archetypal image of Shakespeare's London; the figures placed in the foreground in Southwark resemble actors in a play, drawing us into the life of the city.

Clarkentwell

Smythe Fyelld

Holborne

S: Gyles in the frelde

Charinge Crosse

Suffolke P.   Duresme P.   Savoye   Somerset Place   Arundell P.

Beere howse

The Corte

Pety bridge

Lamberth Marche

The Temple   Why't Freres   Bridwell   Blak Freres   Bents

Paris Garden

Westminster

Steuar Chamber

y' Quenes Bredge

The Slawgh ter howse

Lamberth

Hac es Regia illa totius Anglia ciuitas LONDINVM ad flu-
uium Thamesin sita, Cæsari, vt plures exis timant, Trinobantum
nuncupata, multarum gentium cōmercio nobilitata, exculta domib. ornata tē-
plis, excelsa arcibus, claris ingenijs, viris omnium artium doctrinarumq, gene-
re præstantibus, percelebris. Deniq, omnium rerum copia, atque opum excellētia
mirabilis. Inuehit in eam totius orbis opes ipse Thamasis, onerarijs nauibus per
sexaginta millia paßuum, ad vrbem præalto alueo nauigabilis ————

were officially forbidden in the city, and indeed England, but it seems likely that some were tolerated for the financial services they could offer. The Royal Exchange was opened in 1570, profiting from Antwerp's decline during the conflict with Spain. Thus London's two power centres, governmental and mercantile, coexisted for centuries, often hostile, but mutually dependent.

Westminster owed its importance to the decision of King Edward the Confessor to build a royal palace beside the great abbey of St Peter: here the embryonic offices of the state were established, including the parliament. A social and economic focus was thus created that counterbalanced the City of London; the seat of royal power and justice developed quite distinct from the nation's commercial centre. In time, the Palace of Westminster was overshadowed by Whitehall Palace, seized by Henry VIII from Cardinal Wolsey and steadily enlarged until it became the immense and rambling structure inhabited by the Stuart kings; it would be destroyed by fire in 1698. In both London and Westminster, the 1530s had witnessed a massive transfer of land from ecclesiastical to secular hands following the dissolution of the monasteries. This transfer made the fortunes of scores of families, and gave the royal warrant to a ruthless culture of greed and plunder.

The twin focuses of London and Westminster are clearly demarcated on the maps of the late sixteenth century, but these maps also reveal an obvious third dimension to London's structure, namely the suburbs that were emerging beyond the ancient walls. Outside all the seven gates, clusters of new buildings were pushing into the open fields, filling with new inhabitants, and forming new districts. This development was of great concern to both the city authorities and the Crown, because the people of these districts were outside the jurisdiction of the city statutes, and neither their trade nor their social life could be tightly controlled. The suburbs were feared as possible sources of plague, famine and disorder. A succession of statutes forbade these new buildings, and gave the authorities the right to pull them down. But these statutes proved impossible to enforce, and indeed there was a long-lasting ambivalence in the official attitude to them, for in some ways it suited the city to exclude certain activities from its streets: rendering animal carcasses for glue, brick-making, leather tanning, soap boiling, tin-smithing and so on – all these noxious trades were better left outside the walls, mainly to the east of the city, where the river was both an internal highway and a link with Europe.

The social equivalents of these trades found their home in another suburb, namely Southwark: here, cut off from the city by the river, was a district of notorious prisons, large taverns, pleasure gardens, brothels, bear-baiting pits, and of course theatres. Significantly, the first Globe Theatre had moved there in 1599 from Shoreditch, another district outside the city's jurisdiction. We have to conclude that these suburbs became almost licensed areas of disorder, into which the darker energies of the urban populace could be released. Portia asks Brutus if she is merely his harlot, dwelling in 'the suburbs of your good pleasure', expressing very clearly what these places were like; and yet this particular suburb was the setting of Shakespeare's creative working life.

It would be surprising if London's structures and tensions – physical and social – were not reflected in Shakespeare's plays even outside those set in England. London was a place of royal power, but also of undercurrents of social chaos; in this perhaps it has not changed very much. Royal power might be exercised arbitrarily for good or ill, and disgrace or death might await its victims. That experience, however, offered the chance to display dignity and nobility of character, and contempt for this fickle world, as with the king's victims in *Henry VIII*. A second kind of cruel and arbitrary power was that of the urban mob, which Shakespeare portrayed with horrifying force in part II of *Henry VI*. In one sense of course the rebel Cade, who occupies and pillages London, is the bringer of retribution for the ills of Henry VI's reign, but we are left in no doubt that his bloodthirsty revenge represents a descent into anarchy. The true, unchanging fabric of London's low life appears in the bragging wit, cunning and anti-heroism of the tavern set that gathers around Falstaff. More sordid but less eloquent and less fun are the brothel scenes in *Measure for Measure* and *Pericles*, which must have been based on Shakespeare's own knowledge of the brothels of Southwark, and which are filled with a sense of disgust which cannot be other than personal. But Shakespeare's most specific denunciation of the values of urban life surely comes in Timon's great speech as he looks back at the walls of Athens and takes his leave of the hated city. His betrayal

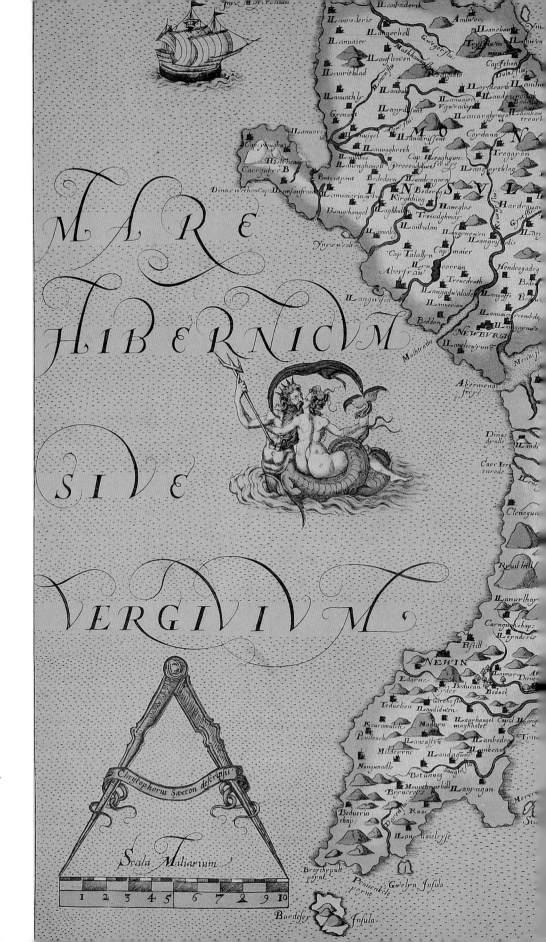

87 The Saxton map of
Caernarfon, Bangor and
Anglesey, 1579. It was at Bangor
Castle that the rebels meet to
plan the division of England
after the removal of Henry IV,
and for this they produce on
stage their famous map.

at the hands of his mercenary friends leads him on to a vision of the city as a place of moral anarchy ruled by wolves, where all is deceit and filth.

Shakespeare displays London as a world of multiple levels: it is the royal focus of the nation's history and identity, but also home to corruption, callousness and a criminal underworld. It is noticeable that nowhere in the plays is there a speech on London comparable to Gaunt's 'sceptred isle' speech on England; this suggests perhaps that, however closely bound to London Shakespeare's life and art may have been, he had no illusions about its danger and its depravity. It is also true that his farewell to the theatre was at the same time his farewell to London, proving that he was not unwilling to retire from the scene of all his triumphs back to Stratford and to silence.

In point of time, the first of the historical plays is *Richard II*, and it typifies the London–Provinces–London rhythm. The play deals only with the final two years of the king's troubled reign. In Ely House, Holborn, the dying John of Gaunt makes his celebrated speech, bitterly critical of the king. In retaliation, Richard seizes all Gaunt's estates and disinherits and banishes his son, Henry Bolingbroke, thus creating the cause of his rebellion. With the resources he has thus pillaged, Richard leaves to quell an uprising in Ireland, and all the middle scenes of the play take place in Wales. We are first shown Bolingbroke in the Severn borderlands, having returned from his exile, mustering an armed force and laying his plans with his allies. Whether it is intended as a symbol or not, he and his party pass the night in Berkley Castle, scene of the gruesome murder of the deposed king, Edward II, some seventy years earlier, and therefore a possible omen of Richard's approaching downfall. The king returns from Ireland, landing in North Wales, to find that his forces have all deserted his cause. It is at Flint Castle that he accepts the inevitable – that he must give up the throne to his challenger. He is taken back to London as a prisoner, and in Westminster Hall amid scenes of great emotion he publicly hands the crown to his successor, now Henry VII. He is then conveyed to the Tower, but then away from London again, to isolation and misery in the dungeons of Pomfret Castle in Yorkshire, until the inevitable murderer arrives to dispatch him.

Bolingbroke had a legitimate claim to the throne, which rested on his descent from King Edward III, and he justified his rebellion as the redress of wrongs committed by Richard. He had, he said, no desire to drench with

88 The Battle of Agincourt, the central event of *Henry V* and of that king's reign, and one that acquired almost mythical status in pre-Tudor English history; from an illustrated manuscript, *c*.1420.

blood 'The fresh green lap of fair King Richard's land',[15] yet clearly he could not be secure while Richard lived. However, in the course of the abdication scene the enormity of the overthrow of an anointed king is bewailed by the Bishop of Carlisle, who prophesied that future ages would 'groan for this foul act', and England become a field of dead men's skulls. The deposition of Richard is the crime, the almost cosmic sin, for which generations of Englishmen will suffer. For his pains the Bishop is arrested for treason, but his words quickly prove true: the final scene of the play takes place in Windsor, where the king is first told that the heads of his slaughtered opponents are en route for London, and he then endures the haunting sight of Richard's dead body brought in before him. Already, only weeks into his reign, he speaks of his anguish and his desire to make a pilgrimage to the Holy Land, 'To wash this blood from off my guilty hand'.[16] There are no battle scenes in *Richard II*: only the king's body lying onstage at the curtain sums up the revolutionary events in symbolic form. The important fact that Richard had no children meant that opposition to King Henry grouped itself around various competing descendants of Edward III.

In *Henry IV* the new king finds little peace, and enunciates the central theme of all these plays with the words, 'Uneasy lies the head that wears a crown.'[17] In both parts of the drama, and in both the main plot and the subplot, the action swings back and forth between London, where the speeches are made, and the outer reaches of the kingdom, where the blood is spilt. Falstaff's dismal career of highway robbery begins and ends at Gadshill, just west of Rochester, on the main road between London and Canterbury. More seriously, the Mortimer–Percy–Glendower rebels are intent on stealing the kingdom. The scene with the map, in which they plan to divide the kingdom between them, occurs at Bangor Castle, and the decisive battle between them and the royalist army is fought at Shrewsbury. Here Falstaff delivers his cynical meditation on honour, plays dead to avoid the action, then claims the glory of having killed Hotspur. Camden gives this brief account of the battle:

> When divers of the nobility conspired against King Henry
> the Fourth with a purpose to advance Edmund Mortimer,
> Earl of March, to the crown as the undoubtful and right heir,
> whose father King Richard the Second had also declared heir

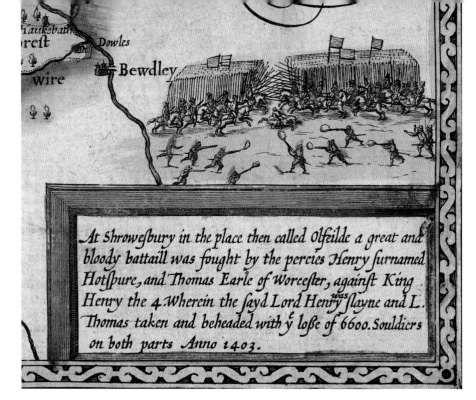

At Shrowesbury in the place then called Olsfilde a great and bloody battaill was fought by the percies Henry surnamed Hotspure, and Thomas Earle of Worcester, against King Henry the 4. Wherein the sayd Lord Henry was slayne and L. Thomas taken and beheaded with ý losse of 6600. Souldiers on both parts Anno 1403.

89 Textual panel on the Speed map of Shropshire, 1611, describing the Battle of Shrewsbury, where the rebels were defeated; these panels are a distinctive feature of the Speed maps not found on those of Saxton.

apparent: and Sir Henry Percy called Hotspur then addressed himself to give the assault to Shrewsbury: upon a sudden all their designs were dashed as it were from above. For the King with speedy marches was upon their back before he imagined. To whom the young Hotspur with courageous resolution gave battle, and after a long and doubtful fight wherein the Scotishmen which followed him showed much manly valour, when the Earl of Worcester his uncle and the Earl of Dunbar were taken, he despairing of victory ran undaunted upon his own death amidst the thickest of his enemies. Of this battle the place is called Battlefield, where the King after victory erected a chapel and one or two priests to pray for their souls who were slain.[18]

In the second part of *Henry IV*, the surviving rebels try battle once more in an obscure corner of Yorkshire named Gaultree Forest. Why does Shakespeare trouble to name it so specifically at the very opening of the scene? This is what Camden has to say about it:

The Forest of Gaultree, shaded in some places with trees, in other some a wet flat full of moist and moorish quagmires; very notorious in these days by reason of a solemn horse-running, wherein the horse that outrunneth the rest hath for his prize a little golden bell. It is almost incredible what a multitude of people conflow hither from all parts to these games, and what great wagers are laid on the horses' heads for their swift running.[19]

So Gaultree was the Newmarket of the north in the sixteenth century, and perhaps its fame had reached even to London. Battle is averted here by a trick played by the royalist commanders, and the rebels go to their deaths. In London itself, Falstaff still reigns at the tavern in Eastcheap, and is now entangled with the picturesquely named Doll Tearsheet; evidently women like Doll were not to be found only in the brothels of Southwark. Significantly, Doll and Mistress Quickly meet their nemesis – they are dragged off by the beadles – in a scene that immediately precedes the downfall of Falstaff himself. Henry IV has died, and, rejected by the newly crowned King Henry V, Falstaff and his crew are carried off in their turn to the Fleet prison. The great comedy is over, the illusion of Falstaff the trickster, the charismatic anarchist, the lord of misrule, is shattered. In the London of the court and noble houses, in the London of the taverns, and in farthest corners of England, the enemies of the king have been broken, and the way is clear for the dawn of a new reign.

In *Henry V* the new king's pressing challenge is to deflect any opposition to himself as the son of an usurper, and to unite the nation. To achieve both these aims, he pursues the classic strategy of identifying an outside enemy to fight – 'to busy giddy minds with foreign quarrels'[20] – and his chosen course is to seek the Crown of France to add to that of England. Three-quarters of the action takes place in France, with the spectacle of the Battle of Agincourt as the real *raison d'être* of the drama. The English force sails from Southampton to the mouth of the Seine, to the strategic fortress of Harfleur, whose siege and surrender inevitably recalls the similar events at Angers in *King John*, which Shakespeare had written two or three years before. During the night before Agincourt, Henry meditates on his high destiny and his duty in terms that are reminiscent of Christ in the Garden of Gethsemane. As king he must sacrifice his private life and his 'heart's ease' so that others may live in peace, and for deep responsibility in sending men to fight and die in wars he advances the theory that the king is here acting as God's representative, for the death that may come to the soldier will be God's judgement on that individual's life. This scene makes explicit the cult and the mystique of kingship which underlie all the history plays. The comic business between the Welsh, the Irish, the Scots and the English has the serious purpose of showing that Henry is the king of Britain, morally towering over all lesser regional rulers.

Agincourt is a testimony to the power which a name, a mere word, may acquire in the imagination: the place itself was nothing, scarcely even a village in the flat fields of Picardy, for the king has to ask the French herald where they are, and receiving his answer he christens the battle 'The field of Agincourt / Fought on the day of Crispin Crispianus'.[21] But this name becomes the symbol which wipes out the shadowy past that lies behind his reign, and it becomes the symbol of the king's power not only to shape historic events, but to redefine the nation's spirit. The action of many years is now telescoped, for it was five years after the battle that Henry married Catherine of Valois, daughter of the French king, in the city of Troyes in June 1420, and was designated heir to the throne of France. In the play it seems a matter of days or weeks, thus linking these events in a strong, purposeful pattern, culminating in glory for the king and for England. And yet it does not, for one of the strangest features of the play is the final speech from the Chorus, who warn that all that has been won will be lost again in the next reign, when England will bleed again. Henry V's glory was a poisoned inheritance, for it depended on his unique character, and could not survive his death, which came just two years later. The first tetralogy of plays closes, and we move forward in time to the second, to the disintegration that awaits.

The Wars of the Roses

HENRY V'S early death had effectively condemned England to years of humiliating defeat in France, and to two generations of dynastic war at home. His son became King Henry VI at the age of nine months, necessitating many years of protectorship, yet even before his minority ended it was evident that his character was as unlike his father's as could possibly be imagined. He was studious, pious and weak, and grew up entirely unable to reign independently from his advisors. Just as Richard's II's lack of a son was the cue for conspiracy and rebellion, so was the personality of the unfortunate Henry VI. Modern historians have reminded us that the years of his reign and that of his successors, Edward IV and Richard III – that is, 1422 to 1485 – did not form sixty years of unbroken civil war. Instead the underlying dynastic tensions broke out periodically into armed conflict. The total time during which private armies were manoeuvring and coming to battle was no more than two or three years. If this is true, we owe the opposite impression very largely to the three parts of *Henry VI*, where the action is compressed in time to give the feeling of a continuous chronicle of warfare, verbal and physical. Although constructed on a framework of fact, the plays present not an exact chronicle, but an epic picture of war.

This compression is to be found in the first play, where scenes with the youthful king alternate with the warfare in France, of which Joan of Arc is the heroine. Joan was active for slightly more than one year, until her capture in 1430, at which time Henry was eight years old.

90 The marriage of Henry V and Catherine of Valois, intended to put an end to all conflict between England and France; from an illustrated manuscript, *c.*1420.

91 Illuminated miniature of King Henry VI and his queen, Margaret of Anjou, receiving the gift of a book, copied from a contemporary manuscript.

The poisonous hatred of the English for Joan of Arc was intense. Here was a young woman who was able, incredibly, to resist that mighty soldier, Lord Talbot, in single combat, a disaster which could only be explained by believing that she was a witch. Later, in a scene before the city of Angers, her capture is made possible by the dramatic desertion of her familiar demons, leaving her helpless. Henry VI's marriage to Margaret of Anjou appears to follow immediately after Joan's downfall, yet it took place in 1445, when he was twenty-four.

The play opens at the funeral of Henry V, followed at once by the news that his conquests are already back in French hands, including the cities of Paris, Rheims and Orleans. The English will launch a counter-offensive in an attempt to retake them, and it is at Orleans, the second city of France, that Joan gains her first great victory when she repels the English and lifts the siege. Even after Joan's removal, the curse remains, however, so that the heroic Talbot meets his death during the siege of Bordeaux, partly because of rivalries and dissension in the English camp, which have become a second curse. In between the stages of Joan's brief career, Shakespeare inserts two vital scenes in England. First is the Temple-Garden scene where rival aristocrats of the houses of York and Lancaster pluck the white and red roses which symbolize their cause. This scene would be celebrated as one of the best-known legends of English history, but there is no warrant for it in the sources Shakespeare used. The second is the scene in the Tower, in which Edmund Mortimer, now on his deathbed, meets his son, the future Duke of York, to rehearse the genealogical claim of the house of York

92 Miniature of Humphrey Duke of Gloucester and his wife Eleanor Cobham, whose misfortunes fill the first half of *Henry VI Part II.* Copied from a contemporary manuscript.

to the Crown. The effect of these two scenes is to prepare us for what would become the Wars of the Roses; but they also project back these dynastic rivalries, showing them as a poison at work in English affairs many years before they erupted into civil war.

These wars do not officially begin until midway in part II of *Henry VI*, located now entirely in England, when the loss of territories in France is widely seen as evidence that England is labouring under some kind of curse. At the same time there occurs the rebellion of Jack Cade and his followers in 1450, a further sign of the anarchy into which England is falling. Both these factors are the cue for the Yorkist rebellion to break out. The scenes when the rebels move from Blackheath into London and the City lies in the hands of the rebels are the most memorable in the play, but it seems certain that Cade's wild, revolutionary rhetoric was drawn from the accounts of the earlier Peasants' Revolt of 1381, to be found in the *St Albans Chronicle*, and repeated by writers such as Holinshed. The murder of the Protector Gloucester, the 'good Duke Humphrey', takes place after the parliament at Bury St Edmund's, but is followed immediately by the death of the men behind the murder. Cardinal Beaufort dies tormented by the demons of guilt, while the Duke of Suffolk is captured by pirates and butchered on the seashore near Dover. The play ends with the first Battle of St Albans, at which one of the combatants laments:

> O war, thou son of hell,
> Whom angry heavens do make their minister,
> Throw in the frozen bosoms of our part
> Hot coals of vengeance! ...
> Henceforth I will not have to do with pity.[22]

93 The Lancastrian kings in the Roses conflict portrayed on the Speed map of Lancashire, 1611.

From London the waves of disorder and death are spreading outwards across the whole country, and the whole of part III of *Henry VI* is an endless panorama of physical violence. The balance of advantage ebbs and flows from side to side, and it is no part of the dramatist's purpose to make us sympathize with one party or the other, yet I think it is his intention to challenge the audience to reflect on wider questions. Why is war good, indeed glorious, when waged in France by Henry V, but now is a curse when waged in England? The Cade rebellion was portrayed as anarchy and Cade as a monster; but why is war waged by peasants any worse than war waged by aristocrats? These questions leap out at a modern audience, but they surely cannot have entirely escaped the Elizabethans either.

HENRY the forth, and first of Lancaster, by a forced resignation and affectioned election, gott the Kingdome, his sone and sones sone succeeded him ED. 4. of York surprised and after him, his sone and Brother raigned, his eldest daughter of Yorke matching with Lancaster ioyned the Red and White Rose in one.

In part III of *Henry VI*, our war-weariness might easily have reached its height at the Battle of Towton, in Yorkshire, except that Shakespeare evokes much of the horror of it tangentially. Fought amid flurries of snow on Palm Sunday 1461, it was perhaps the bloodiest battle ever recorded on English soil, in which over 60,000 men took part, of whom almost 30,000 were killed. The old chroniclers said that the blood of the slain lay frozen on the ground until the thaw came, when it ran in rivulets along the ditches for a distance of several miles. Nominally the victory went to the Yorkists and Edward IV, but like all the victories it was temporary, and there would always be another battle. The battle scenes are memorable for several episodes away from the fighting. Firstly, King Henry has been identified as a presence that always brings ill fortune, and therefore he spends the time while the fight is raging banished from the action, alone and lamenting the tragic state of his kingdom, wishing he were a simple shepherd without power or responsibility. He then witnesses a son who has unknowingly killed his own father in the battle, and then the reverse, a father who has unknowingly killed his son, these two figures summing up the special horror of civil war. Secondly, when the battle is over, the victorious Yorkists find the body of the Earl of Clifford, one of their most inveterate enemies, and talk to his corpse, attempting to goad it into life so that they may kill him again more lingeringly. The enormity

94 The Yorkist kings in the Roses conflict portrayed on the Speed map of Lancashire, 1611.

95 Norden's Map of Westminster, 1593, showing the nobles' houses by the riverside – Leicester, Arundel, Somerset, Savoy, Russell – where many of the scenes in the York–Lancaster plays take place.

of the holocaust at Towton seems to have deterred any contemporary artist from making pictures of it.

Towton was not the end, however, and ten years later, in 1471, this phase of the struggle was finally concluded at the Battle of Tewkesbury, which, says Camden, 'is a great and fair town, having three bridges to pass over, standing upon three rivers, famous for making woollen cloth, and the best mustard, which for the quick heat it hath, biteth most and pierceth deepest'. But after this homely picture, he moves on to the grimmer reasons for the town's fame:

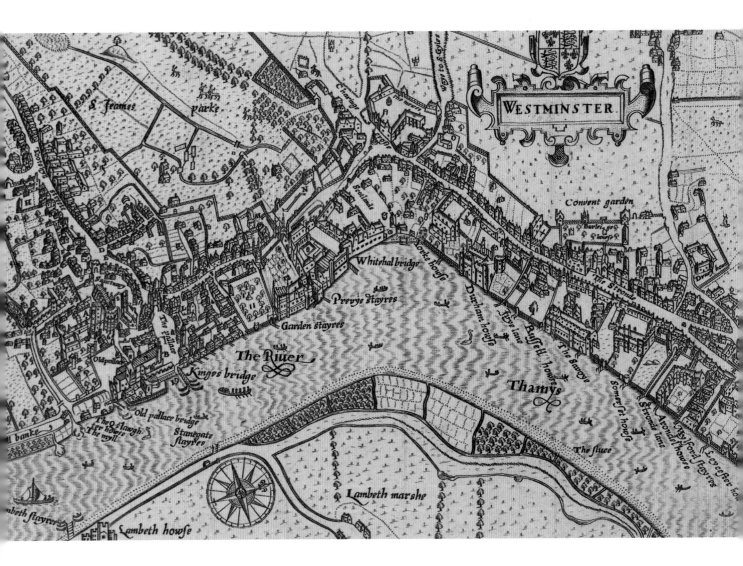

Neither is this town less memorable for that battle whereby
the House of Lancaster received a mortal wound: as where
very many of their side in the year 1471 were slain, more taken
prisoner and divers beheaded, their power so weakened and
their hopes abated, especially because young Prince Edward, the
only son of King Henry VI, a very child, was there put to death
and in most shameful and villainous manner, his brains dashed
out, that never after they came into the field again against King
Edward IV.[23]

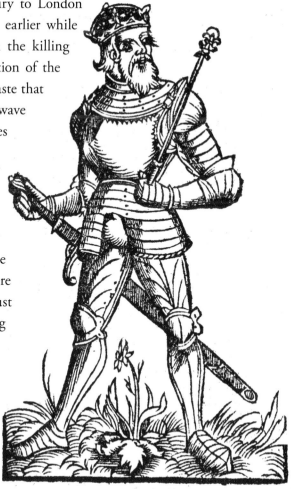

96 A king in battle armour,
from Münster's *Cosmographia*,
1552.

This drama of unremitting bloodshed ends with King Edward's light-
hearted words, 'For here, I hope, begins our lasting joy.'[24] That joy will lead
into the reign of Richard of Gloucester, soon to be Richard III. Gloucester's
last act in *Henry VI* was to ride hurriedly from Tewkesbury to London
to murder King Henry in the Tower. To have killed him earlier while
his son still lived would have achieved nothing, but with the killing
of Prince Edward, Henry's death will complete the extinction of the
House of Lancaster. Gloucester leaves Tewkesbury in such haste that
King Edward does not see him go, and again we see the wave
movement between the distant provinces, where the battles
take place, and London, the seat of power.

An interval of time clearly passes between the end of
Henry VI and the opening of *Richard III*, during which
Richard waited and schemed for the crown, which he was
to wear for just two years. *Richard III* commences only
when it becomes clear that King Edward is dying. Almost the
whole of the play is set in London, for it is in London where
the personal power struggle among those of royal blood must
be played out. Richard creates the impression of a cunning
spider at the centre of his web, picking off his enemies one
by one. There are two brief excursions out of the city to
show the execution of some of them: in Pomfret those
of Rivers, Grey and Vaughan, and in Salisbury that of
his former ally, the Duke of Buckingham.

Richard, for all his malevolence, was always accounted a fearless soldier, and his end came on the

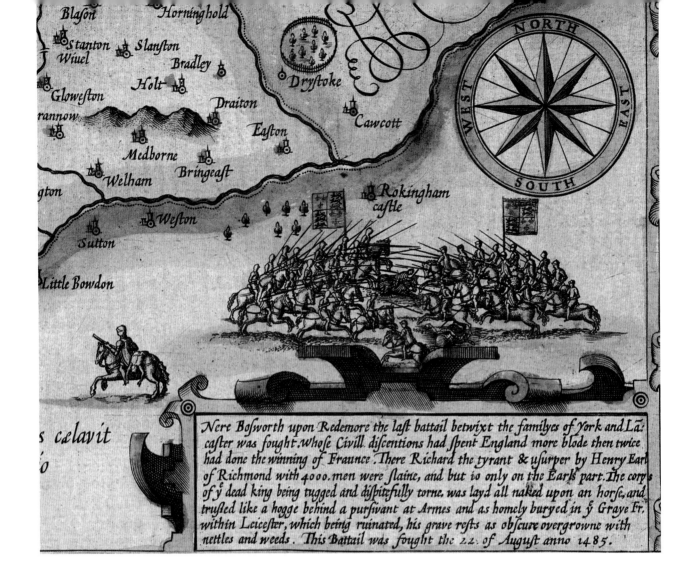

Within the map image:

Blaſon
Horninghold
Stanton Slanſton
Wiuel
Bradley
Gloweſton
Holt
Draiton
rannow
Easton
Cawcott
Medborne
Welham
Bringeaſt
Weſton
Sutton
Little Bowdon
Dryſtoke
Rokingham
caſtle

NORTH
WEST
EAST
SOUTH

s cælavit
o

Nere Boſworth upon Redemore the laſt battail betwixt the familyes of York and Lā-
caſter was fought.whoſe Civill diſcentions had ſpent England more blode then twice
had done the winning of Fraunce. There Richard the tyrant & uſurper by Henry Earl
of Richmond with 4000.men were ſlaine, and but 10 only on the Earls part. The corps
of ỹ dead king being tugged and diſpitefully torne, was layd all naked upon an horſe, and
truſſed like a hogge behind a purſivant at Armes and as homely buryed in ỹ Graye Fr.
within Leiceſter, which being ruinated, his grave reſts as obſcure overgrowne with
nettles and weeds. This Battail was fought the 22. of Auguſt anno 1485.

97 Panel from the Speed map of Leicestershire describing the Battle of Bosworth and the death of Richard III. It was indeed in the former Greyfriars Churchyard in Leicester that Richard's bones were finally unearthed in 2012.

battlefield, naturally far from London. This is how John Speed described the Battle of Bosworth, in a text placed upon his map of Leicestershire:

Nere Bosworth upon Redemore the last battail betwixt the familyes of York and Lancaster was fought, whose Civill discentions had spent England more blode then twice had done the winning of Fraunce. There Richard the tyrant & usurper by Henry Earl of Richmond with 4000 men were slaine, and but 10 only on the Earl's part. The corps of the dead king being tugged and dispitefully torne, was layd all naked upon an horse, and trussed like a hogge behind a pursivant at Armes and as homely buryed in the Graye Friars within Leicester, which being ruinated, his grave rests as obscure overgrowne with nettles and weeds. This Battail was fought the 22 of August anno 1485.[25]

Richard's evil character was talked about and written up immediately after his death, and his physical deformity was interpreted as evidence of his demonic nature. One historian, John Rous, endorsed the story that Richard was 'held for two years in his mother's womb, emerging with teeth and with hair down to his shoulders'. He was 'small of stature, with uneven shoulders, the right being higher than the left'.[26] The legend of this monster evidently made him the personification of the madness that had disfigured England for a generation. Yet we must also remember that Richard had grown up in this terrible war zone and what he was, others had made him.

It is fitting that this blood-soaked figure should mark the end of the Wars of the Roses, and that the new age dawns in the person of Henry Tudor, who is described in almost Christ-like terms. Yet his claim to the throne was more slender than any of the combatants in those wars, for it came through his mother, who was a great-great-granddaughter of Edward III. Therefore the reality behind the kingship ideal remains deeply enigmatic. Of the six English kings in the historical cycle which Shakespeare constructed covering the century between Richard II and Richard III, three were removed by rebellion and put to death, while in every reign there were challengers who believed that they themselves should be king: this does not sound like a quasi-sacred view of the king's figure, not a divine-right theory. But evidently there was an alternative theory of the state available. The king was the state, and all authority and power resided in him; but there was a pragmatic sanction that if he were unworthy in some way, he might be removed. The man who removed him must be the new king – that is the crucial point: it was the ideal of kingship that stood as the bulwark against the anarchy which England experienced briefly in the Peasants' Revolt and in Cade's rebellion. This was the theory; whether it stood up as a justification for what England experienced during these civil conflicts, Shakespeare does not tell us overtly, but I suspect his answer would be that it did not.

98 (*overleaf*) 'I do not like the Tower of any place', says one of the doomed princes; the Tower of London acts as a symbol of royal power and tyranny in *Richard III*; surveyed by Hayward and Gascoigne, 1597.

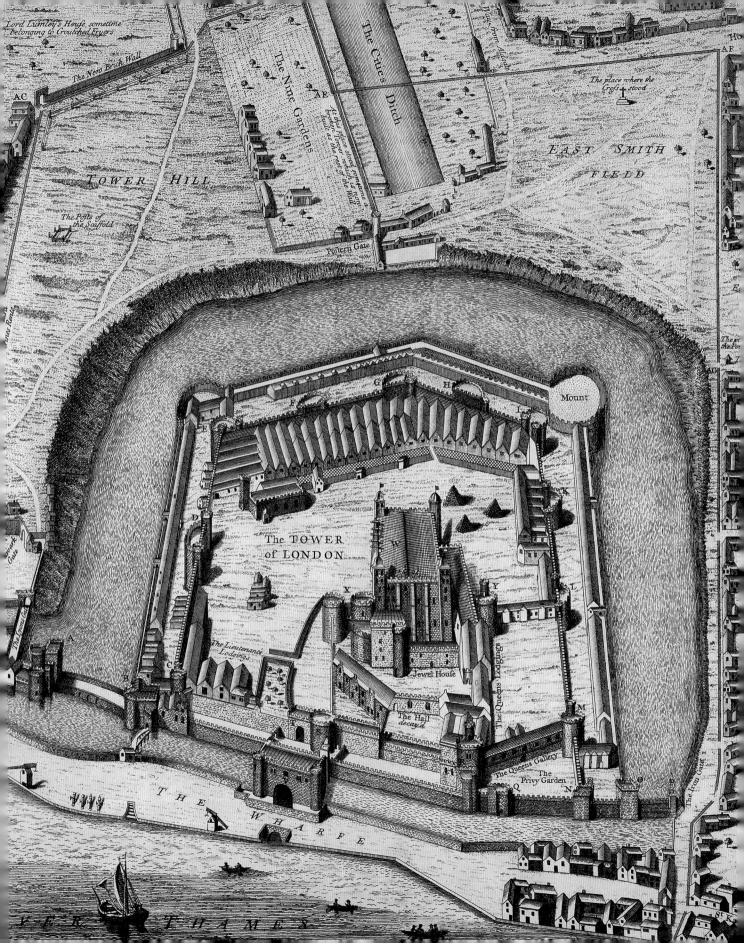

Lord Lumley's House, sometime belonging to Crutched Fryers

The New Brick Wall

AC

TOWER HILL

The Posts of the Scaffold

The Nine Gardens

AE

In this place stood sometime a tower which is now built as the rest of the Wall.

The Cities Ditch

Postern Gate

Ways from Aldate

The place where the Cross stood

EAST SMITH FIELD

AF

Ho

Ee

AG

The pi the Por

G   H

F

E   Mount

D   K

The TOWER
of LONDON   W   Y

X   The Queens Lodgings   L

James Ravins

Tower Gate

The Tower Gate

A

The Lieutenants Lodgings   Jewel House

C   The Hall
                                          decay'd

B

M

The Queens Gallery
The Privy Garden

Q   N

The Iron Gate

THE WHARFE

St.K

VER THAMES

Two isolated plays

THE LAST ROYAL play is *Henry VIII*, but forty years separates it from the final scenes of *Richard III*, and it is as much an outrider after the age of the dynastic plays as *King John* is before it. *Henry VIII* is a very different kind of play, in which the king does not appear to be the emotional or moral centre. Instead it is part-chronicle, part-pageant, showing the relationship of the king to half a dozen key figures in turn: the Duke of Buckingham, Queen Katherine, Cardinal Wolsey, Anne Boleyn and Thomas Cranmer. Of these, the first three fall fatally from the king's grace, and the motto of the play might well be the ancient principle 'The prince's anger is death.' After the play ends, of course, they will be joined by a fourth victim – Anne Boleyn. The action is almost wholly in London, as with *Richard III*, and for the same reason: that London is the centre of the nation's governmental power and of all the attendant political and personal rivalries. We also see a banquet scene in York Place, home of Wolsey, which would be taken over by King Henry and renamed Whitehall Palace, as someone in the play explains: 'You must no more call it York-place, that's past / For, since the Cardinal fell, that title's lost / 'Tis now the king's and call'd Whitehall.'[27]

There is one significant scene outside London, namely when the tragic figure of Queen Katherine, now rejected and isolated, has left London to spend her last days at Kimbolton House in Huntingdonshire. Here she experiences her dream vision, in which she sees a number of angels who offer her garlands, perhaps of beatitude or martyrdom. It is significant

99 (*overleaf*) The coronation procession of Edward VI from the Tower to Westminster in 1547, one of the few depictions from this period of London's streets.

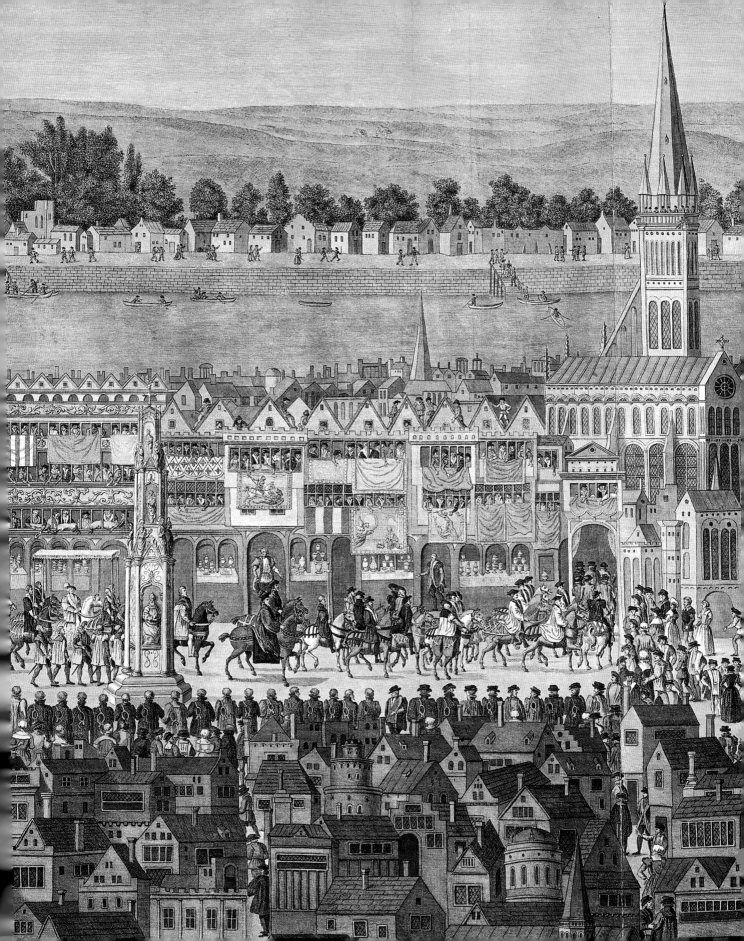

BEATVS vir qui non abiit
in confilio impiorum, & in via
peccatorum non ftetit, & in cathedra pe=
ftilentiæ non fedit.

100 Manuscript
miniature of Henry VIII
in a relaxed moment,
reading before he goes
to bed, or perhaps before
he starts his day, c.1540.

that this scene occurs far from the court, far from London with its taint
of human duplicity, trial and sorrow. Kimbolton thus becomes by contrast
a place of retreat and spirituality. In its mystical religious feeling, this is
unlike any other scene in Shakespeare, and it has given support to the
possibility that he may have been a crypto-Catholic, as some scholars have
conjectured. The final scene of the play is the christening of the baby
Elizabeth in the palace – but which palace? There is no indication in the
text, but as the future queen was born at Greenwich Palace, as her father
was also, the probability is that Greenwich is intended.

With *Henry VIII* we reach the end of the chronicles of the English kings;
but where does this play leave the Tudor myth? Securely vindicated in an
age of glory? Perhaps, for Henry evidently has the strength of character
to hold the kingdom together in unity and civil peace, and to stifle any
possible thought of challenging his fragile claim to the throne. But his
peace comes at a price, and the play might be read as a telling indictment
of a megalomaniac. Henry breaks all the rules, betrays his closest allies at
will, plays ducks and drakes with relationships, with conscience and with
law. His career represents, in the words of commentator James Spedding,
'Little else than the ultimate triumph of wrong'. What lesson should we
learn from this – that the king makes the rules, that he defines right and
wrong? A century after King Henry's death, a civil war would be fought
over this principle, not with the familiar aim of replacing the king, but with
that of abolishing kingship altogether. This would have been unthinkable
to Shakespeare and his contemporaries. To them, faith in the mystique of
kingship was absolute, but they could not avoid the question posed in these
plays: how often does history produce a king worthy of that faith?

In *The Merry Wives of Windsor* we reach another ending – the end of
an imaginary journey from the ancient near east and a time 2,500 years
before Shakespeare lived, to domestic, small-town comedy in an England
recognizably that of the Tudor age. True, the principal character is Falstaff,
whom Shakespeare had killed off very publicly, supposedly around the year
1413, very soon after the coronation of Henry V, the king who rejected him
and broke his heart. We were told that Bardolph and Nym followed Falstaff
to their deaths in the French war in 1415, but they too are resurrected, and
the leap of 180 years to 1595 can be seen as mere poetic licence, for most

VINDESORIVM

amoenissimus: aedificia m
& illustris Garetterior

Depingebat
SEPTE

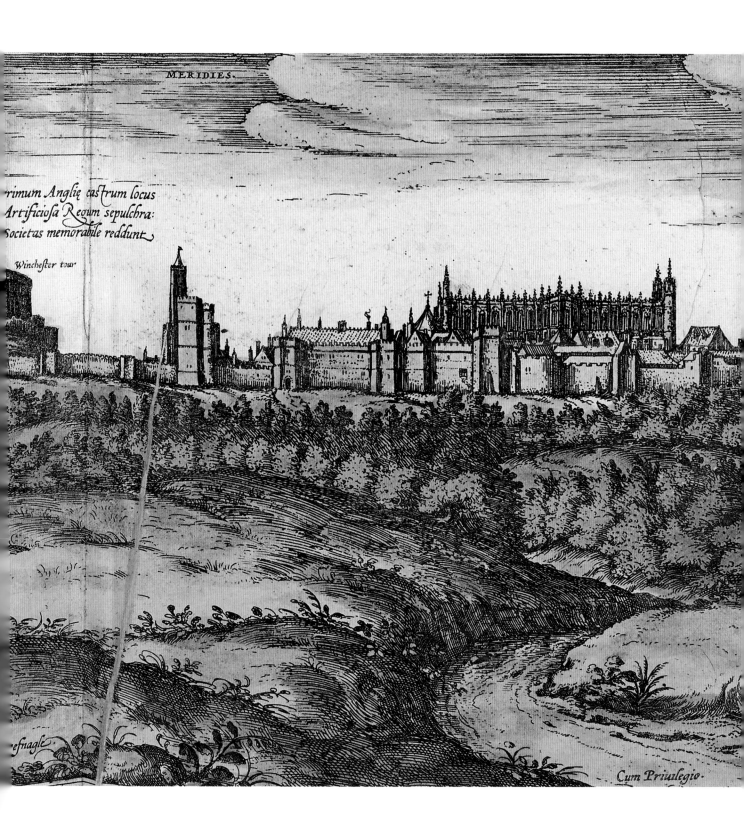

MERIDIES.

rimum Angliæ castrum locus
Artificiosa Regum sepulchra:
Societas memorabile reddunt

Winchester tour

efnagle.

Cum Priuilegio.

101 (*previous spread*) Windsor,
from Braun and Hogenberg,
1575, with figures who might
easily be the Fords, the Pages
and some others like Fenton,
Slender, Evans or Caius too.

people agree that in *The Merry Wives* we are seeing the nearest thing that
Shakespeare wrote to a play set in his own country and his own time. The
famous story that the play was written at the request of Queen Elizabeth
herself, because she wished to see Sir John Falstaff in love, has no real
authenticity, and in any case that is what we do not see. We do not see
love but a cynical pretence of love behind which lies merely lust and the
pursuit of money, for this Falstaff is a very different man from the comic
genius of *Henry IV*, and certainly a lesser figure.

Nevertheless the connection with Queen Elizabeth may be real, and it
may explain the central question why the play should be set in Windsor
rather than in any other town in England. This is another of those
Shakespeare plays which have no single literary source, but there was a
rich tradition of Italian stories about cuckolding which the dramatist was
certainly very familiar with, from Boccaccio onwards. Sometimes the plot
works out at the expense of the unfortunate husband, but sometimes it
is the lover who is foiled and humiliated. *The Merry Wives* clearly begins
as a story of this kind, but in its later scenes it turns into something very
different, for here we are given a magical, ceremonial spectacle, in which
Falstaff's duplicity and lust are not merely exposed but ritually punished.
Scholars now think it virtually certain that this part of the play has a
hidden contextual meaning, namely that it was commissioned as an enter-
tainment for the ceremony of an investiture of the Order of the Garter. The
origins of that Order lie in the idea of purity of thought, and a play that
castigates lust and treachery would express its central creed. The Garter is
mentioned quite specifically in the final act, while the fairies' song, 'Fie on
sinful fantasy', condemns lust and all unchaste desire. Early in 1597, Lord
Hunsdon, the Lord Chamberlain, and the patron of Shakespeare's theatre
company, was made a member of the Order, and it is thought that the play
was written to celebrate his investiture, and performed either in Windsor
or London, or perhaps both.

The play is certainly set in the real Windsor, for the castle and the
Thames are mentioned, and Eton and Datchet; but it is the final scene in
the park and forest that is most significant. Here Falstaff is tricked into
disguising himself as that figure of Windsor legend, Herne the Hunter, the
one-time keeper of the forest who hanged himself at Herne's Oak, and who

is now a malignant spirit who stalks the area wearing horns and rattling his chain. Falstaff's donning of the horns symbolizes his miserable failure to cuckold Ford or Page, and his exposure as a cheat. There is also a clear echo of the story of Actaeon, the hunter who was transformed into a stag by the goddess Diana, and torn to pieces by his own hounds. All these references and layers of meaning made Windsor the only place where the play could be set. So this apparently simple domestic comedy, which feels loose and unfocused in structure, turns out to be a surprisingly complex interweaving of bourgeois farce, supernatural countryside traditions, and regal ceremony. The fairies make a clear link with Shakespeare's other forest play, *A Midsummer Night's Dream*, as does the subplot concerning the troubled wooing of Anne Page by her competing suitors. It is a play which is of Shakespeare's own country and time, but which sets up resonance of other ages, other lands and other literary traditions. *The Merry Wives of Windsor* may not be Shakespeare's greatest play, but it is one that shows his imagination at work on a very diverse range of materials, and, as we enter into this realm of the imagination, it makes us, the audience, 'Take upon 's the mystery of things / As if we were God's spies',[28] which is perhaps the unique achievement of all his work.

102 Greenwich Palace shown on the Wyngaerde panorama of London, *c.*1544. It was the birthplace of both Henry VIII and Queen Elizabeth I, and is therefore the presumed setting of the final scene of *Henry VIII*.

Notes

PRELIMINARY

1. *Coriolanus* 3.3.133.
2. John Livingston Lowes, *The Road to Xanadu: A Study in the Ways of the Imagination*, New York, 1927, book I, ch. 1, p. 1.
3. *Much Ado About Nothing* 2.1.273–282.
4. *Richard II* 4.1.92–100.
5. Christopher Marlowe, *Tamburlaine the Great, Part II*, 5.3.150.
6. John Donne, 'An Anatomy of the World', 1611.
7. *King Lear* 3.2.1.
8. *King Lear* 1.2.1–20.
9. *The Tempest* 5.1.57.

PART ONE

1. John Speed, *A Prospect of the Most Famous Parts of the World*, London, 1627, p. 11.
2. *Julius Caesar* 5.5.76.
3. *Antony and Cleopatra* 4.13.70–71.
4. *Antony and Cleopatra* 1.1.39–40.
5. *Julius Caesar* 4.3.329.
6. James Boswell, *Life of Samuel Johnson*, 11 April 1776, London, 1791.
7. Speed, *A Prospect*, p. 3.
8. *Othello* 5.2.409.
9. *Othello* 5.2.411.
10. Charles Hughes (ed.), *Shakespeare's Europe: Fynes Moryson's Itinerary*, London, 1902.
11. Richard Hakluyt, *Principal Navigations, Voyages and Discoveries of the English Nation*, London, 1904, vol. 6, pp. 2–3.
12. Abraham Ortelius, *The Theatre of the Whole World*, London, 1606, p. 90.
13. Speed, *A Prospect*.

PART TWO

1. Abraham Ortelius, *The Theatre of the Whole World*, London, 1606, p. 2.
2. Hondius & Jansson: *Atlas, or a Geographicke Description of the World*, Amsterdam, 1636, p. 42.

3. *Othello* 1.3.162–163.
4. *The Merry Wives of Windsor* 1.3.37–39.
5. Hondius & Jansson, *Atlas*, p. 42.
6. Ibid., p. 371.
7. Ibid., p. 376.
8. *Henry VI, Part III* 3.2.193.
9. *Much Ado About Nothing* 1.1.58.
10. Niccolò Machiavelli, *The Prince*, ed. Quentin Skinner and Russell Price, Cambridge, 1988, p. 52.
11. Christopher Marlowe, *The Jew of Malta*, prologue, 14–15.
12. Charles Hughes (ed.), *Shakespeare's Europe: Fynes Moryson's Itinerary*, London, 1902, p. 135.
13. Ibid., p. 421.
14. Ibid., p. 423.
15. Ibid., p. 415.
16. Ibid., pp. 132–5.
17. Ibid., pp. 117–18.
18. Ibid., p. 160.
19. Ibid., p. 406.
20. *Edward II* 5.4.31–36.
21. Hughes (ed.), *Shakespeare's Europe*, p. 408.
22. Ibid., p. 411.
23. *A Winter's Tale* 5.2.99.
24. *A Winter's Tale* 5.1.185.
25. *Twelfth Night* 2.1.1–2.
26. *The Taming of the Shrew* 3.1.6–9.
27. Arthur Brooke, *The Tragical History of Romeus and Juliet*, London, 1562, prologue.
28. *The Two Gentlemen of Verona* 2.3.6.
29. *Hamlet* 3.2.184.
30. Fynes Moryson, *An Itinerary...*, 1907 edn, vol. 1, pp. 123–4.
31. *Hamlet* 1.4.80.

PART THREE
1. *King Lear* 4.1.44–45.
2. *Richard II Part II* 2.1.40–52.
3. *Henry VI Part III* 2.5.73–75.
4. *Love's Labour's Lost* 5.2.920–925.
5. *Henry VI Part II* 4.8.1.
6. *Henry IV Part I* 1.2.43–44.
7. William Camden, *Britannia*, trans. Philemon Holland, London, 1639, p. 651.
8. *Cymbeline* 3.1.19–20.
9. *Cymbeline*, 3.1.26–29.
10. Raphael Holinshed, *The Chronicles of England, Scotland and Ireland*, London, 1808.
11. Ibid., p. 294.
12. Ibid., vol 2, pp. 294–5.
13. *King John* 4.3.12.

14. Edward Hall, *The Union of the Two Noble and Illustre Families of Lancastre and York*, 1548.
15. *Richard II* 3.3.47.
16. *Richard II* 5.6.56.
17. *Henry IV Part II* 3.1.34.
18. Camden, *Britannia*, p. 596.
19. Ibid., p. 723.
20. *Henry IV Part IV* 4.5.217–218.
21. *Henry V* 4.7.80–81.
22. *Henry VI Part II*, 5.2.38–41, 61.
23. Camden, *Britannia*, p. 359.
24. *Henry VI Part III* 5.7.48.
25. John Speed, *A Prospect of the Most Famous Parts of the World*, London, 1627.
26. 'Historia Regum Angliae' in G. Bullough, *Narrative and Dramatic Sources of Shakespeare*, 8 vols, London, 1957–75.
27. *Henry VIII* 4.1.119–121.
28. *King Lear* 5.3.16–17.

Bibliography

Boswell-Stone, W.G., *Shakespeare's Holinshed: The Chronicle and the Historical Plays Compared*, London, 1896.

Braun, G., and Hogenberg, F., *Civitatis Orbis Terrarum*, 6 vols, Frankfurt, 1572–1617.

Bullough, G., *Narrative and Dramatic Sources of Shakespeare*, 8 vols, London, 1957–75.

Camden, W., *Britannia*, trans. Philemon Holland, 1610 and 1639.

Hadfield, A., *Shakespeare and Renaissance Politics*, 2004.

Hadfield, A., and Hammond, P., *Shakespeare and Renaissance Europe*, 2004.

Hall, E., *The Union of the Two Noble and Illustre Families of Lancastre and Yorke*, 1548.

Harvey, P.D.A., *Maps in Tudor England*, Chicago, 1993.

Holinshed, R., *The First Volume of the Chronicles of England, Scotland and Ireland...* 1577, reprinted in 6 vols, London, 1807–08.

Hondius & Jansson, *Atlas or a Geographicke Description of the World*, Amsterdam, 1636.

Hughes, C., (ed.), *Shakespeare's Europe: Fynes Moryson's Itinerary*, London, 1902.

Livingston Lowes, J., *The Road to Xanadu: A Study in the Ways of the Imagination*, New York, 1927.

Machiavelli, N., *The Prince*, ed. Quentin Skinner and Russell Price, Cambridge, 1988.

Miola, R.S., *Shakespeare's Reading*, Oxford, 2000.

Münster, S., *Cosmographia*, Basel, 1544; illustr. edn 1552.

Münster, S., (ed.), Claudius Ptolemy: *Geographia*, Basel, 1540.

Ortelius, A., *The Theatre of the Whole World*, London, 1606.

Speed, J., *The Theatre of the Empire of Great Britaine*, London, 1611.

Speed, J., *A Prospect of the Most Famous Parts of the World*, London, 1627.

Sugden, E.H., *A Topographical Dictionary to the Works of Shakespeare and his Fellow Dramatists*, Manchester, 1925.

Tooley, R.V., *An Atlas of England and Wales: The Maps of Christopher Saxton*, London, 1979, facsimiles.

Tyacke, S., and Huddy, J., *Christopher Saxton and Tudor Mapmaking*, London, 1980.

Turner, H., *No Mean Prospect: Ralph Sheldon's Tapestry Maps*, 2010.

Woodward, D., (ed.), *The History of Cartography*, Volume 3: *Cartography in the European Renaissance*, Chicago, 2007.

Picture credits

Index

WESTMINSTER

West to S. Gyls

the mewis

Yorke howse

bridge

Durham house

Fyve lane

Ruffell howse

The Sauoye

Thamys

The sluce

Convent garden

Burleige howse

The Stronde

Drury how

Somerset house

Stronde lane

Arondell howse

Weyford stayres

Leycester howse

Temple

marshe